DATE DUE

MAY 07 2001	
DEC 20 2005	

IntraActive Therapy

IntraActive Therapy

A Practical Approach to Effective Short-Term Treatment

by

Carl Mumpower, Ph.D.

KRIEGER PUBLISHING COMPANY

MALABAR, FLORIDA

1992

Original Edition 1992

Printed and Published by
KRIEGER PUBLISHING COMPANY
KRIEGER DRIVE
MALABAR, FLORIDA 32950

Library of Congress Cataloging-in-Publication Data

Mumpower, Carl.
IntraActive therapy: a practical approach to effective short-term treatment/Carl Mumpower.—Original ed.
p. cm.
Includes index.
ISNB 0-89464-611-7 (alk. paper)
1. Brief psychotherapy. I. Title.
[DNLM: 1. Psychotherapy, Brief—methods. WM 420 M9617i]
RC480.55.M86 1992
616.89'14—dc20
DNLM/DLC
for Library of Congress 91-7070
CIP

10 9 8 7 6 5 4 3 2

CONTENTS

Acknowledgments vi

Introduction vii

1. An Emphasis on Practicality 1
2. Understanding the Individual 9
3. Assessing the Individual 17
4. Treating the Individual 27
5. Intervention Methods 43
6. Keys to Successful Short-term Intervention 49
7. The Therapeutic Process 57
8. Some Practical Therapy Concepts 65
9. Making a Good Thing Better—Practical Therapy Issues 87
10. From the Client's Perspective 111
11. A Quick Reference Guide to Psychotherapeutic Medications . . 119
12. Conclusion 129

Appendix A Patient Intake Information 131

Appendix B Sentence Completion Inventory 133

Appendix C The IntraActive Psychological Inventory (IPI) 135

Appendix D Recommended Readings 141

Bibliography 143

Drug Reference Bibliography 146

Index 147

ACKNOWLEDGMENTS

I would like to express thanks to Don Boone, a social worker, Patricia Emerson, a psychologist, and Bob Rigdon, a counselor, for their good help through the years. Don, your enthusiasm, love, and sense of the absurd have been a continued inspiration. Patricia, your support, gentleness, and noncompetitive spirit have been a model and help through trying times. Bob, your acceptance, practicality, and insight helped get me started.

I am so glad to have known these three distinct personalities from three differing disciplines. Each functioned in unique fashion, yet their commonality was always evident. They are a continued reminder to me that as therapists, we are much more alike than different.

INTRODUCTION

I believe that being a therapist is to be part of one of the most exciting professions of our time. No one could possibly have more stimulation, opportunity, and variety of involvement. That is not to say it is easy. On the contrary, the training, the challenges, and the responsibilities are extraordinarily demanding.

Many things contribute to the enjoyment of the therapist's role, but few have a greater impact than an understanding of how to do it well. A measure of this competence can occur naturally, but most people do not gain their skills and knowledge alone. There have been many individuals involved in my own growth and development. I look back with appreciation to my studies under psychologists, social workers, psychiatrists and counselors. Each discipline taught me important things about understanding and helping people. All of the hours of theory and practice, sometimes conflicting and confusing, gradually developed into a model of understanding and intervention that made sense and worked.

I have often wondered if the path needed to be so long and arduous. Although there is no doubt that I have benefited from everything I have learned, I have many times questioned the efficiency of the process. The substance was always there, but it seemed to take so much searching to pull it out. Therefore, I have concluded that my preparation was more diverse than necessary. I am convinced that a person can become an effective therapist in much less time than tradition dictates, and that all that we learn, while beneficial, is not always necessary or functional.

This book is designed for therapists in training and therapists in practice who are looking for a frame of reference that is structured, practical, and understandable. The foundation for this effort is simple—we all think, feel, and do. Each of these elements is active within every person, and most forms of psychological dysfunction center on one or more of these internal forces. Almost every successful therapeutic approach addresses the thinking, feeling, and doing selves in some fashion. **IntraActive Therapy** is focused on helping the therapist accomplish this intervention on a more intentional, direct, and short-term basis.

IntraActive Therapy emphasizes the inner person, is based on a system of threes for ease of understanding, and keeps a dynamic focus on action as a source of problem resolution. In developing **IntraActive Therapy** I have pursued three primary goals:

1. To establish a clear, effective, and quantified therapy model that has broad application to mainstream therapeutic needs;
2. To provide a practical therapy approach that attempts short-term intervention with an eye toward cost, time, and resource management.
3. To offer a flexible therapy approach incorporating core techniques characterized by ease of definition, training, and implementation.

IntraActive Therapy is designed to be applicable to the majority of problems a therapist may encounter. The framework is adaptable, easily personalized, and allows for convenient interface with alternative approaches. While simple in design, I believe that **IntraActive Therapy** can match the effectiveness of many therapeutic methodologies that are more complex or training intensive.

A therapist is an individual who helps other people address life problems through psychological intervention. It is readily apparent how diverse this role can be. Some therapists work in hospitals and deal with severely dysfunctional people. Others work in peer support centers, schools, or outpatient clinics which present different but equally demanding problems and issues. It does not take a Ph.D. to be an effective therapist any more than it takes an M.D. to provide attention to most physical problems. The depth and scope of training necessary depend entirely on the nature of the life problems a therapist will address. With this in mind, **IntraActive Therapy** has been developed for therapists at varying levels of training and experience. It has practical application for the experienced doctorate level therapist, as well as for a lay counselor working in a spouse abuse center.

IntraActive Therapy training places greatest emphasis on the common problems that will be encountered, not the atypical and exceptional.

IntraActive Therapy should not be the only therapeutic framework learned. It will better serve as a beginning foundation for a therapist in training, or a centering frame of reference for the experienced therapist. In either case, **IntraActive Therapy** is not the end of your search for knowledge, but the beginning. It is a good beginning, one that will send you well on your way to becoming a more effective therapist.

CHAPTER 1

AN EMPHASIS ON PRACTICALITY

INTRODUCTION

No matter what the human endeavor, people have always sought ways to do it more quickly, more effectively, and more cheaply. The food people eat, the airlines they fly, and the cars they drive are all products of this same process of development and evolution. The nineties will bring similar change to therapeutic services. Out of necessity and demand, therapy will become short term, task efficient, and cost effective (Lewis, 1991). This evolution will not occur without failures and resistance, but it will occur. There is no choice. There are simply too many people needing psychological help, and too few resources to provide it (Visotsky, 1991). Practicality will be the therapeutic model of the nineties.

In the beginning, therapy was an experimental science understood by few and practiced on a limited number of people. Some were helped and some were harmed by their therapy experience, but the collective base of knowledge began to grow. Other educators, scientists, and healers were stimulated to explore the psychological makeup of people and ways to address their problems (James, 1908). With time, more efficient, definable, and broadly applicable theories of intervention were developed. It was during this period that therapy evolved from being merely another experiment into a true science of action.

Until the fifties, therapy was still a service largely reserved for those with catastophic illness, those who were wealthy, and those in proximity to urban settings. Almost every therapeutic model developed prior to this time involved long-term and training intensive methods that precluded mainstream application. Many therapy models were practiced as an art as well as a science. The therapist's talents were not easily transferable or even definable (Allport, 1968). In any case, the masses of people perceived therapeutic services as an intimidating form of magic that should be reserved only for those who were crazy or dangerous to the public good.

Over the past several decades, however, attitudes and emphases have changed (Malan, 1976). People want to live better materially, physically, and psychologically. Thus, there has been an increasing desire amongst the mainstream of people to pursue answers to problems that heretofore were ignored or denied. People do not have more problems, but they do have a greater awareness and interest in addressing their problems. This evolution, while exciting, has overwhelmed the health care system. A huge and growing share of health care dollars is spent on psychological interventions, and the number of people pursuing therapy is increasing markedly. For these and other reasons, the majority of therapeutic services of the future will be provided on a brief basis utilizing methodologies that are practical, content specific, and goal oriented (Barten, 1971). This is the motivation and framework for **IntraActive Therapy**.

Short-term therapy will not and should not be the only type of therapy available. Older models that have stood the tests of time and experience will continue to serve a valued role. For the majority of people, however, short-term methods will prevail because they are more efficient. The field of psychological intervention began as an experiment and became a science and art form. Therapy for the nineties will be more a matter of specific skill and practical application.

RECONSIDERING THE MYTHS

IntraActive Therapy emphasizes short-term therapy methods. Short-term therapy attempts intervention in a matter of weeks, typically six to eight, rather than months or years. This model of intervention is relatively new, and that which is new can be threatening. Myths have evolved around short-term therapy that do not fully match the realities. It will help if you can lay these myths aside and give your attentions to the more legitimate applications and limitations of short-term intervention methods.

Myth No. 1—Short-term therapy is not effective with serious problems.

The opposite is probably true. The more serious the problem, the more intentional the intervention should be. Brief therapies go after problems in an aggressive manner, with concrete emphasis on problem definition and intervention. It is true that short-term methods applied to very serious problems may not work on a short-term basis. In almost all cases, however, they will work more quickly and efficiently than longer-term methods that are less intentional. Serious is usually a matter of depth of entrenchment versus complexity. The harder and faster you dig, the sooner you are going to get there, no matter how deep the hole needs to be.

Myth No. 2—Short-term therapy restricts the therapist and limits the therapeutic outcome.

Short-term therapy guides and supports you, the therapist, toward successful intervention. Any type of guide, by definition, places restrictions. This is acceptable as long as constructive desired results are obtained. It is limiting, in that there are constraints of emphasis and time, but these limits serve as a means to an end. There is no therapy method so restrictive as one that does not work. Short-term therapists are house painters not artists. You may not produce any major works of art but you offer a functional, productive, and beneficial contribution.

Myth No. 3—Short-term therapy is dehumanizing and rarely personalized to individual need.

Anything that helps a person be more functional is profoundly humanizing. Whereas it is true that short-term methods cannot always help a person find his or her fullest potential, these methods can very specifically teach a person how to find it for himself or herself. Short-term therapy is about helping people live their own lives. Through an emphasis on the positive, practical, and concrete, it is a change methodology that has very broad application to the human experience. Short-term therapy is one of the more people oriented therapy methods because it is designed to be pragmatic and temporary.

Myth No. 4—Short-term therapy produces results that do not last.

Short-term does not mean superficial. One car accident that lasts five seconds can leave an emotional impact lasting a lifetime. Because short-term interventions are typically concrete and practical, they are more easily understood and generalized. Consequently, the long-term results can be greater than longer-term interventions that are not as easily internalized. The key to successful intervention is the power to reach and teach a person. Time is only one of many forces that will effect this outcome.

Myth No. 5—Short-term therapy is designed for minimally trained or unskilled therapists.

Many people are taught to believe that the more complex something is, the more superior and intellectually sophisticated it is. Perhaps, but most people drive a four door sedan to work rather than a cute sports car, and they do so because of reliability and efficiency. The real world functions through that which is definable and practical and carries its own weight. The smartest person seeks to do things as efficiently as possible. Short-term therapy is comparatively easy to understand and learn, but these factors are assets not limitations. Training levels should be determined by the task at hand, not arbitrary standards of superiority.

THE VALUES AND LIMITATIONS OF SHORT-TERM THERAPY

This book is centered on one approach to short-term therapy, and will demonstrate a decided bias for this intervention method. Yet, no treatment modality provides all the answers to all of the questions. **IntraActive Therapy** is no exception and anyone who reads this book should be cautioned against myopic thinking. My effort is to help you, the therapist, narrow your therapeutic effort toward the pragmatic, while broadening your thinking to the other potentials that surround you.

I have included a list of values and limitations associated with short-term therapy. Less than complete, each list will help strengthen you as a short-term therapist. No matter what the tool, you need to know what it can not do as well as what it can.

Values

- Cost, time, and resource efficient.
- Definable and quantitative in structure.
- Practical, goal oriented, and geared toward here and now.
- Applicable to variety of therapy contexts.

- Real-world emphasis.
- Simplified training requirements.
- Interfaces well with other methodologies.
- Compatible with current trends in third-party reimbursement.
- Demonstrated effectiveness with mainstream psychological problems.
- Highly suited to retraining, supplemental training, and initial training under resource constraints.

Limitations

- Produces increased initial client anxiety.
- Allows for limited processing and relationship evolution.
- Can facilitate oversimplification of problem issues.
- May encourage some therapists to exceed their knowledge and training.
- Abuse potential by reimbursement providers, employers, and others who may overemphasize financial constraints over individual need.
- Not ideally suited to all therapeutic conditions—some disorders may respond better to other methodologies.
- Training as a short-term therapist can be misused as a replacement for diverse training and education exposure.
- Can be utilized as a therapy of image versus substance.
- May be exploited as a trendy therapy method and misused by untrained individuals.
- Sometimes misunderstood as a therapy method that uses long-term techniques in a short-term context.

As you develop your skills as a therapist, remain aware of these values and limitations. Remember that becoming an effective short-term therapist is not the end of your training, but a good beginning.

BECOMING AN EFFECTIVE SHORT-TERM THERAPIST

This book will teach you how to become an effective short-term therapist. When you have read it, you will have been exposed to a quick and solid battery of information on the "how to's" of short-term therapy. You will have the information, but this, alone, will not make you a therapist. What you do after you finish this text will determine that.

Becoming a good therapist requires a list of ingredients beyond titles and degrees. There are a number of important components that can help make you a productive and helpful agent of change. As you work to become an effective therapist, make sure you consider the following factors:

Knowledge

Before you can be functional at something, you have to know what to do and how to do it. That is knowledge; that is why you are reading this book; and why you will continue to explore other information resources throughout your life.

Energy

Therapy is not easy on either side of the table. As an effective therapist, you will recognize that coasting, or low energy involvement, will limit the outcome of your efforts. Therapy takes a strong investment of energy to produce a strong impact.

Compassion

Some people are easy to care for and others are not. You will not be able to help anyone significantly unless you can care about that person. People in pain are not always pleasant, but if you can look through compassion beyond their defenses, you can then help establish new directions and hope.

Courage

It takes courage to risk a psychologically intimate relationship with another person. It is hard to confront another person's defenses and help redefine important aspects of his or her life. It takes risk to open oneself to rejection and the many unknowns that are a routine part of any therapeutic process. A therapist with courage is willing to enter a human arena that cannot otherwise be faced.

Self

As therapists you do not have to be perfect human beings. You do need to have a working understanding of who you are and make efforts toward self-betterment. Clients will look to you for strength, example, and hope. Having a good sense of yourself will help you meet their needs.

Support

As a therapist you will need a strong support system. This system will involve logistical support, in the form of an office and such, as well as emotional support in the form of supervision and peer involvement. If you maintain a good support system, you help insure your effectiveness and continued availability. Neglect it, and you will be a candidate for professional burnout and ineffectiveness.

Success

To feel good about what you do you need evidence of success. Sometimes this evidence comes in the form of client appreciation, peer recognition, or a good professional income. Many times, however, your sense of success will have to come from within. You will have to recognize your own good efforts and credit your account accordingly.

Flexibility

People are anything but static. If you set your perceptions and attitudes in concrete, then you will have difficulty keeping up with your clients. A good therapist is able to evolve with current realities and adapt where prudent and helpful. If you can bend, then you will have a longer reach of effectiveness.

Perceptiveness

You cannot effect change in something you do not know about. Your clients will tell you much of what they know, but that can be only a small part of their reality. You will have to be sensitive to other possibilities, using your senses to see that which might otherwise be overlooked. Listen with all of yourself and you will increase your perceptiveness. Do that, and you magnify your effectiveness as a therapist.

Passion

Passion is a word normally reserved for romance, yet it is also applicable to your focus. A good therapist will approach therapy with enthusiasm and excitement. There will be somber and quiet moments, but even these can be met with passionate sensitivity. It is difficult to be good at anything in life without first having some joyful and passionate appreciation of what life is all about.

Now you have a sense of what your task requires, let's take a closer look at the core of **IntraActive Therapy**. During your exploration, you will learn to apply the principles of short-term therapy, make the best use of your resources, emphasize the practical, and be brief in your efforts. The framework you need is here and will help you well on your way to becoming an effective short-term therapist.

CHAPTER 2

UNDERSTANDING THE INDIVIDUAL

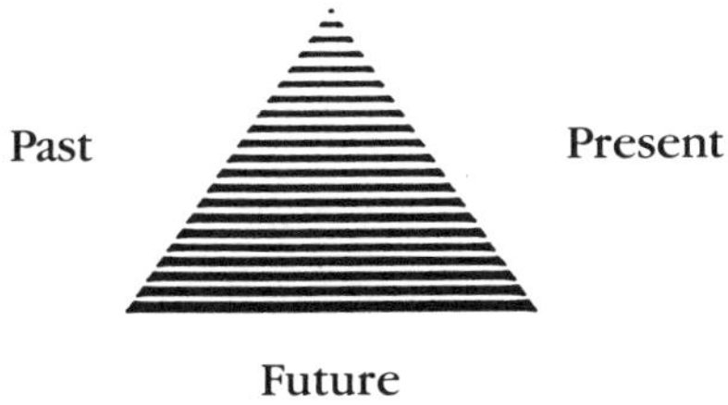

INTRODUCTION

To bring about change in an individual, you must first have an understanding of why people are the way they are. **IntraActive Therapy** conceptualizes people in the context of their **past**, **present**, and **future**. Each lends important insights into why people think, feel, and do in their own unique way.

THE PAST

A person's past is the most reliable measuring instrument for understanding that person. What happens in infancy, youth, and adolescence certainly lays the foundation for the future. If the past is filled with painful, difficult, and damaging events, then future lives will be negatively affected. There are many approaches to assessing individuals through their past, but for your purposes you will focus on three primary areas. More than most, these three play powerful roles in the development of individuals.

Parents and Upbringing

From the moment people come out of the womb, who they are is mostly in the hands of their parents. Their security, nourishment, affection, and guidance come to them through their parents' efforts. If those efforts are good ones, then they are likely to respond accordingly. If they are not, emotional scars can develop (Wolff, 1989).

Parents impact on children in many ways. Their **model**, for example, has a very powerful influence on how they live their own lives (Erickson, 1968). Although most children duplicate the more powerful models in their family, sometimes they react in another direction and reject them. Either way their parents' model is important in that they are reacting for or against what they are exposed to. Everything that parents do is a statement of what they think their children should do. Their work habits, social patterns, attitudes, values, and lifestyle in general are a billboard that teaches children, for better or worse, what they should be.

Children learn to **love** themselves by being loved by others. If their parents do not give them the affection they need in their youth, they then have trouble loving themselves. Life is a difficult process, and the support of self-love and love from others goes a long way to making it easier (Glasser, 1965). Further, when people are not taught to care for themselves, they have trouble loving others. In fact, they probably do not love other people any more than they are able to love themselves.

Children cannot successfully raise themselves. They need direction, encouragement, and resources. An absence of this **guidance** inhibits their collective development. The gaps that result are the source of much of the dysfunction and emotional pain that people experience in later life. A child is like a garden that must be cultivated to reach its full potential. Parents are not able to guide their children to any greater level of development than they possess themselves.

Parents have a key role in a person's past. Their **models**, their **love**, and their **guidance** set the stage for much of an individual's future.

School and Peer Involvements

Second to parental influences as a key issue of the past are individuals' school and peer involvements. In the formative years (0–5), parents are a dominant force. Beyond this point, social and school involvements become of progressive importance (Adler 1956).

The reasons are simple. It is at school that children acquire their most diverse exposure to the "how to's" of life. Parents may show them the way, but school usually provides the place to practice. Children are continually exposed to thinking, doing, and feeling issues in an environment that demands independence If they are prepared for these demands prior to their school years, then their transition is likely to be a good one. Most school environments are, in fact, designed to be reasonably supportive. If children do not enter the school arena with the necessary foundation, then their experiences there will be less positive.

As a learning environment, school provides opportunity for successes and failures. Relationship skills, academic abilities, and physical talents are continually put to the test. If children do not measure up, the impact on their self-image can be devastating (Glasser, 1965). Being unpopular, athletically clumsy, or scholastically marginal does not endear children to their peers. Furthermore, these failings do marked damage to their personal sense of value.

Experiences with **peers** is an important part of school life. Fundamental relationship skills are formed by how children are able to interact with their schoolmates (Minuchin, 1974). Positive or negative relationship experiences and patterns in school tend to carry on into adulthood (Wolff, 1989). The seemingly innocent and simple interactions of children on a playground are deceptively powerful. Futures are made and broken there and as children relate to one another, they set patterns that can last a lifetime.

Successes, or their lack, are another important part of school and peer experiences. Successes breed self-acceptance and acceptance from others (Mering et al, 1957). They teach about abilities and capacity for improvement. They encourage growth and creativity. In the absence of a variety of successful endeavors, it is the rare child who leaves school with a positive sense of self.

The most diverse exposure to adults occurs in school. Teachers are second only to parents in the time they spend with children and in the influence they carry. Teachers who work at **nurturing** and **endorsement** can enhance the parents' efforts and go a long way towards compensating for gaps that may exist. Conversely, unnurturing and critical teachers can have a terrible impact. The adult support received in school teaches children what to expect from the world that waits for them when they, too, become adults.

Children go to school not just to learn facts. They go to learn about people, themselves, and life. Lack of achievement in any of these areas sets a poor stage for their future. Much of what people do or do not do as adults can be traced to the gaps or failures that occur in their school years.

Identity Formation

A third critical aspect of the past is the formation of an identity (Erickson, 1969). Depending on exposures, people can come out of childhood with a good sense of self, a poor sense of self, or little or no sense of self. As one might expect, parents, teachers, and peers have the greatest impact on identity formation. The key components of that identity are the **values**, **knowledge**, and **skills** that are taught.

Values are people's rule book. Values set the standards, potentials, and limits of their lives. Spiritual teachings are an important part of value formation. If positive and workable values are taught, then chances for life success are enhanced (Glasser, 1965). Conversely, if taught that being selfish, dishonest, or nonproductive is OK, then interfacing with the real world will likely be difficult. Identity comes mostly from success, and good values will usually lay the groundwork for success (Lewis, 1991).

We live in a diverse world. Knowing about that world and how to live in it effectively is the essence of identity. This kind of **knowledge** does not occur naturally. It must be developed intentionally. Everything from knowing how to hold a fork to how to greet another person helps mold identity. Knowledge voids leave identity voids.

Talent is nice, but skill is better. Talent is luck of the draw, but skill can be developed. Skills and developed talent help mold identity. Usually the greater the **skills**, the greater the sense of self. Constructive past experiences are ones that leave people with more skills than they started with.

It is rare that the impact of the past is overemphasized. But with all its power, the past does not need to dictate the future. A past is a foundation not an ending. What people do today and tomorrow determines that.

THE PRESENT

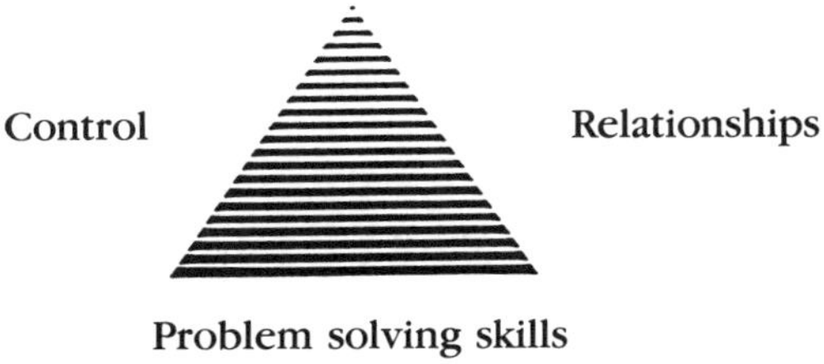

The past, present, and future are all significant to understanding individuals. Yet, it is the present that has the greatest impact. What is happening in people's lives right now, this moment, is what is most important to them, and ultimately one of the therapist's better paths to understanding who they are (Fagan and Shepherd, 1970). In terms of the present, a sense of control, relationships, and problem-solving skills stand out in importance.

Control

People like to have control. With control comes a sense of comfort and security (Sonnenburg et al., 1985). Without that control, life has a tension that can interfere with the ability to function and enjoy. In trying to understand people and their need for control, the issues of external control, internal control, and adaptability are significant.

Our culture emphasizes the importance of **external control**. From childhood, people are taught that having control of their environment is a must for happiness. Too little control, and they fear becoming victims (Bergman, 1985). They live in constant anticipation of being harmed by some outside force. Too much control, they become corrupted and lose touch with other life priorities. Too, they live in a tense state because keeping control of their outer world is so difficult. Finding a balance between too much and too little external control is an ongoing process for most people.

Internal control is de-emphasized in our culture. People may be excellent at managing the world around them yet give little thought to managing the person within. Identity, self-appreciation, and emotional stability all come from internal control. Having a sense of understanding and power over inner self seems to be every bit as important as external control over their environment (Perls, 1969).

External and internal control are not fixed realities. They ebb and flow with time and events. Thus, people must also have the capacity to **adapt** and be sensitive to the evolution of control. There is so little that is permanent in an average existence that they either learn to adapt or stay constantly frustrated in their efforts to maintain a sense of stability. The pursuit of control and the capacity to adapt to changing internal and external forces is what life is all about.

Relationship Factor

People need people. They offer models of how to live, keep others in touch with reality, and provide comfort and nurturing that cannot be duplicated elsewhere. The nature of people's relationships with others can tell much about who they are and why they are that way.

The relationship with **self** is probably the most important of all (Rogers, 1951). The level of self-support, acceptance, and awareness plays a major role in helping people deal with the present in a functional and enjoyable way. A good relationship with self does not seem to occur naturally, however. It is generally a result of learning, and this can occur at any life stage. In the absence of a good relationship with self, everything about life is harder. There is greater susceptibility to hurt from others. Also, people are more prone to mental illness, and are less able to handle the difficulties encountered in day-to-day living. If individuals do care about who they are, they then have an inner friend to accompany them as they travel through life.

Families are also very important. Old wounds and hurts, present day breakups, conflicts, and dysfunctional patterns of interaction can undermine the unique support that families provide (Morawetz and Walker, 1974). More positive family relationships can give people a source of backup, encouragement, and love that helps push them forward. Many of the general problems that people have can be traced to their current family relationships (Minuchin, 1974).

Other relationships at large serve a good purpose, too. Everything, from a superficial encounter with a grocery clerk to friendships with co-workers, serves as support. People need people, and healthier lifestyles will usually contain a good variety of relationships at all levels. When people do not bond with each other, the resulting loneliness can have a decidedly negative impact on the quality of life.

Problem-Solving Skills

Although life can hold much joy, it also carries its share of problems. An individual who can face these problems in a productive manner lives out his or her life from a position of strength and security (Phillips and Wiener, 1966).

In solving problems, one of the first skills people draw on is their capacity to **reason**. They must think in order to recognize a problem, define it, and explore solutions. Reasoning is a skill that must be taught and practiced. Many people in society do not possess good reasoning skills, and thus have difficulty solving the problems they encounter in day-to-day living. Being at the mercy of external forces, these people will be more prone to dysfunction and maladaptive coping methods as they seek to avoid and defuse problems they are not able to solve themselves.

Problems and conflicts dissolve with time but can do tremendous damage in the interim. It takes courage to face some problems, and there is always some element of **risk** involved. Many people abhor risk. They fear their own vulnerability and forego taking chances. This fear, in turn, leads to a paralysis of self that limits success in solving life's problems.

Maturity is also important in problem solving. Selfish attitudes, vindictive actions, and angry obsessions can undermine accountability and the ability to solve problems (Glasser, 1965). Many people assume a reactive position to problems, doing what comes naturally rather than exploring other responses that may work best. Flexibility is a creative process that comes from **maturity**. Although some maturity comes from aging, most is developed through individual effort.

The ability to solve problems is important to maximum individual functioning (Polansky, 1971). If a person cannot solve problems, then he cannot function in a healthy fashion. There are simply too many blows in life for the average individual to absorb.

THE FUTURE

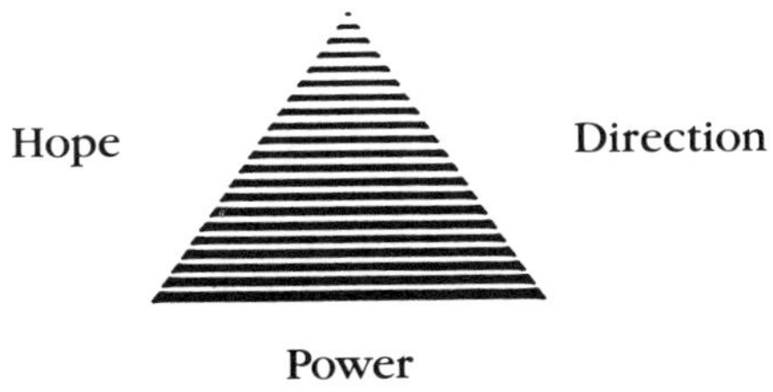

The future, though undetermined, can be influenced and improved. People can, to some extent, prepare for tomorrow and through today's actions set the stage for what is to come. They can not fully control their future, but they can turn the odds in their favor.

Just as what everyone is today can influence tomorrow, the image of tomorrow can impact on today. At its best, that image should offer hope, set directions, and give a sense of power.

Even the most uninformed knows that if people live through the moment, another moment comes. Insuring that moment and having some sense that it will be a good one is important to most people. They need the **hope** that the future holds promise and meaning (Rabkin, 1977). Take that hope away, and enthusiasm for life falls by the wayside. Hope is one of the most basic emotional needs. Some people are able to maintain hope with only a sliver of support. Others find hope difficult to maintain even in the face of good events. It is not that they do not appreciate the good that they have, rather life experiences have left the impression that the good will be taken away. Take away hope and you rob the essence of the individual.

Because the future is an unknown, goals and **directions** aid in the ability to face what is ahead. Those who struggle toward tomorrow without some plan of action, are more likely to go forward hesitantly and stumble on the way (Phillips and Wiener, 1966). Direction does not determine people's future, but it does bend it in their favor. It is important because it offers them some sense of influence over their own destinies. When they look toward tomorrow, people face a question mark. The size of the mark can be reduced by the goals and directions that are established today.

In understanding people it is important to note their sense of future personal **power**. Usually, the more that power develops from the inside, the better. If the power rests too much with others or outside events, then they live in greater fear and discomfort. To obtain complete power is impossible. Something is always intruding. Nevertheless, a personalized sense of ongoing power is a necessary ingredient for happiness. Much can be learned about people by noting the strength of their sense of personal power.

CHAPTER 3

ASSESSING THE INDIVIDUAL

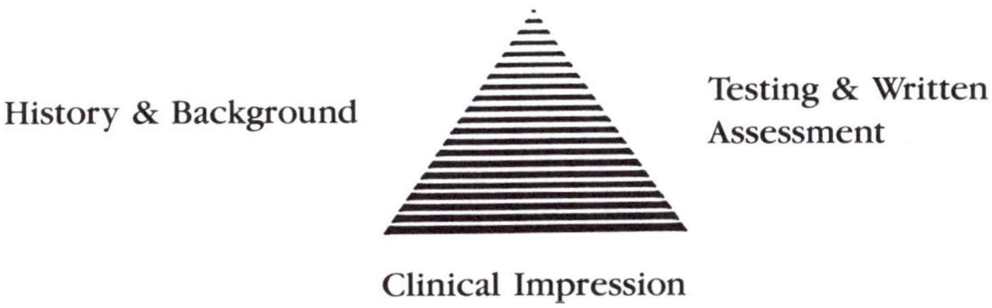

INTRODUCTION

Once you have established a basic framework for understanding people, your task is to apply that understanding to the individual. You begin this process through a client assessment. Time and ongoing contacts will flesh out your initial work, but it is possible to develop a good base of insight into a person during the early stages of therapy. You can more ably accomplish this goal by actively pursuing history and background information, utilizing objective tests and assessment tools, and developing helpful clinical impressions.

OBTAINING HISTORY AND BACKGROUND

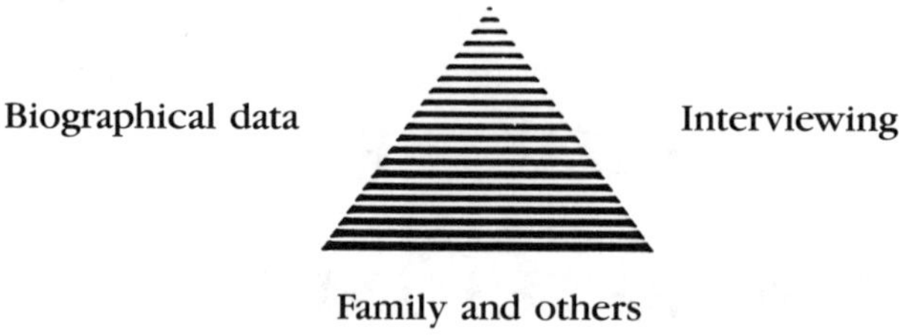

Biographical data

Biographical data is simply factual information that is relevant to the client. There are numerous ways to obtain this information, including a form on **intake information** that is completed by the client prior to the initial session (see Appendix A). This form should ask questions that address academic history, age, family status, health status, treatment history, symptoms, and other information that will assist you in your assessment efforts. People respond to these sorts of questions with surprising honesty. Opening up on paper also helps them warm up prior to the verbal disclosure that will occur in the initial session.

Checklists, which can be part of the intake information form, help to elicit information. Rarely will individuals check symptoms that they do not have, and, in fact, a checklist can be a reminder of problems they may tend to overlook. If you develop your own checklist, keep it simple and use everyday language. Most people will not understand the term *cyclothymic*, but they will understand mood swings.

A significant part of the first session should be devoted to obtaining an **informal history** of the client. Exploring an individual's background helps you to understand, but also establishes a relationship bond (Gustafson, 1986). When people share with you, they feel closer. Your warmth, receptiveness, and nonjudgmental responses will be keys to their willingness to disclose. Most historical data is collected on a chronological basis. Significant areas to explore would include, but not be limited to the following (Wolpe, 1990):

1. Birthing circumstances—normal delivery? complications?
2. Parental status—1 parent or 2? adoption?
3. Health—problems? disabilities? limitations?

4. Parents style—permissive? authoritarian?
5. Siblings—rivals? close?
6. Day-care—how much? quality?
7. Memories—earliest? general flavor?
8. Developmental process—normal? snags?
9. Peer relationships—best friends? types?
10. School—important experiences? how many?
11. Successes—when? how often?
12. Failures—how many? impact? cause?
13. Activities and involvements—type? value?
14. Environmental issues—neighborhood? home?
15. Support systems—family? neighbors?
16. Models and examples—major? role they played?
17. Important events—impressions? impact?
18. Puberty—physical problems? trauma?
19. Social skills—source? effectiveness?
20. Academic achievement level—grades? effort?
21. Future plans—realistic? constructive?
22. Significant life experiences—trauma? impact?
23. Identity—source? nature? substance?
24. Regrets—scope and depth? accuracy?
25. Major relationships—number? quality?

In exploring a client's history, it is generally not necessary to follow a question/answer format. This approach can feel rigid and actually discourage disclosure. You are better advised to let the dialog flow in a relaxed conversational manner, although the interaction may jump around and seem fragmented. One moment you may pick up information about an individual's past and the next may focus on today. As the interaction continues, the puzzle pieces will generally fall into place. You may have to nudge and prod a bit to juggle loose some information, but by the time most people come to you they want to open up and share. They do not understand what you need to know or what is important, however, and you will have to provide some direction.

Interviewing

Interviewing is the foundation of the therapeutic process. Each time you sit down with a client you are participating in an interview of sorts. A successful interview will help you establish a relationship, obtain information, and in some way have an impact.

Trust and confidentiality are prerequisites to the successful interview. Having taken the steps to come to you has already laid some basis of trust. Keeping it alive requires that you continue affirmation of the client's original decision to let you in. Clients instinctively trust people who they feel are genuinely concerned. (Glasser, 1965). Your attention to an individual, which can include everything from offering a cup of coffee to providing your home phone number for emergencies, can send a message of concern. Inside the most defensive and withdrawn person on earth is the buried desire to be cared for. He has simply lost faith in the ability to find such caring. If you can commit yourself to showing real concern for the clients you see, then you will be feeding their trust. Self-disclosure and openness on the therapist's part can also encourage trust. Your model says that you are willing to risk and trust them which supports their desire to do the same.

Clients come to you for more than professional expertise. You are a person they can open up to in confidentiality. They can tell you important and hurtful things that will go no further. That sense of confidentiality is crucial to the successful interview. You will not learn what you need to learn unless the client/patient believes that information will not travel beyond your office.

Open communication means you will learn more about the individual. Not everyone knows how to be open and you may have to show the client how. Let the client know that the more he shares, the better you can understand and help. Encourage the client to tell you anything that he believes you should know, especially those concerns that are difficult to share. The tough disclosures are often the best disclosures, but that will not be known unless you enlighten the client. Each interview should provide some opportunity for an individual to tell you something about himself. Important information may not come out at first. However, an open door to open communication will improve the chances for significant disclosure over time.

Some therapists feel more comfortable with a **formal** therapist/client relationship. They believe that formality keeps boundaries intact and is less threatening to the patient. There is merit to this perspective, but I personally feel more comfortable with an **informal** interview style. It seems more natural, and people respond better to what they are used to. Whichever style you prefer, keep in mind that formal does not mean cold and rigid, and informal does not mean slack and unintentional. The successful interview will be handled in whatever way best facilitates your information gathering efforts. Do what works.

Family and Others

The individual will be your best source of information, but you should also address other resources. Family members, teachers, and employers can provide you with insight that a client may not have. An accurate assessment will rarely occur in an information void.

Family members are typically one of your best and most available information sources. Regular and open discussions with parents, spouses, and siblings can provide alternative perspective to your own impressions that you receive from the client. The information you receive from family members is not always accurate, but it is coming from a source that is involved with your client on an intimate basis. Even if their information is biased, contact with family members still helps you understand a major force in your client's life (Bowen, 1978). You get a chance to see their models, support system, and family dynamics up close. Considering the importance of families in a person's life, this exposure can be indispensable.

You should also have access, when possible, to **work and school** information resources. Time at work and school is real life and can tell a great deal about one's level of functioning (Minuchin, 1974). Not only are work and school involvements typically some of the healthiest daily contacts, successes or failures in these areas can have strong influence on behaviors. Confidentiality and privacy issues will not always make this possible, but these resources should be cultivated where possible.

Essentially, any **significant other** should be considered as a potential assessment resource. A primary physician, a previous therapist, a close friend, or the referring party may have insights that can help you in your assessment efforts. You must be sensitive to the confidentiality boundaries and take care not to disclose the client's involvement in therapy without permission. When that permission is available and contact with a signifi cant other is appropriate, your chances for a balanced and accurate assessment are substantially increased.

TESTING AND WRITTEN ASSESSMENT

Psychological testing is a constructive source of information in client assessment. The usefulness of this resource is sometimes overemphasized, and it is important to consider testing as only one of your assessment tools. Testing does have advantages. Used properly, it can lend objectivity to the assessment process. Many people are curious about psychological tests, trust their accuracy, and assign them magical value, and thus, willingly open up to the test (Patterson, 1966). In addition, responding to a piece of paper can sometimes be less threatening than face-to-face contact.

Informal inventories are one of your testing resources. These can include sentence completion tests you make up yourself (see Appendix B), informal inventories that assess various aspects of the individual (see Appendix C), or other test that gather personal information. These tests tend to be less formal and statistically valid than tests that are empirically based and researched. On the plus side, informal inventories are usually brief, practical, and nonthreatening. With cautionary enthusiasm for the data they provide, you can gain good insights through these instruments.

A second testing resource is **objective personality tests**. These tests typically require more extensive therapist training, are time consuming, and produce data that is difficult to assess. Many of these tests can be computer scored which can enhance objectivity and limit assessment inconsistencies. Although this group of tests is considered objective, this is not always the case. Highly complex projectives have much room for interpretation. Outside these concerns, objective personality tests typically have a reasonable level of statistical validity and reliability that offers some assurance of accuracy.

A final group of tests would be those that are targeted to a specific area. Instruments that address careers, learning disabilities, intelligence, aptitudes, and abilities fall under the definition of **targeted tests**. These tests are helpful in that they are specific and narrow in their focus. Targeted tests can help you round out your base of information on a area of particular concern.

A therapist should have some expertise on the "how to's" of testing. However, you are generally advised to not administer a test unless you know how to use it. Successful testing is part science and part art. Leave the more complex tests to those who have been trained in their use and do such testing on a regular basis. Nonetheless, do not be afraid to try testing as an assessment resource. There are a wide variety of simple, brief, and valuable tests available that the average therapist can use with a measure of confidence.

Clinical Impression

Your final assessment tool will be that of clinical impression. This is simply the process by which you pull together your knowledge base, powers of observation, and intuitive senses to draw conclusions about your client (Pittenger, 1960). Although this is a qualitative process, this does not mean that objectivity is absent.

Many of your initial clinical impressions will come from what you **hear**. Make an effort to really listen to what your client is saying to you. Listen to the surface words, but also the deeper meaning that may be there. Think about what is being said as you listen. Apply your knowledge base and pay attention to the conclusions you may draw. A computer may be objective, but it cannot begin to hear the things that you can.

What you **see** can also tell you a great deal. A person's appearance, body language, and visible reactions can offer meaningful information. Use your eyes intentionally. Search for insights that can help you help the person. Important information quite often may be missed because a therapist simply does not pay attention to the visual cues that are presented.

Then, there is this factor called **instinct**. It works and will be one of your best assessment tools if you learn its value and limitations. There is nothing wrong with instinctive reactions, as long as those impressions are not set in concrete. Using your total self to sense and understand is a routine part of day-to-day living and certainly has professional application. When you have instinctive impressions, it is often wise to check them out with your client. He may be surprised by the accuracy of your insight, or discard it now, but deem it true at a later point. Use your gut instincts as you would any other part of your assessment. Compare them to your other resources and keep question marks at hand, because your instincts can be wrong. Remember, this is true of *any* of your assessment tools. The diversity of your resources, as well as the process itself, ensure a high probability for accuracy.

PROBLEM ASSESSMENT

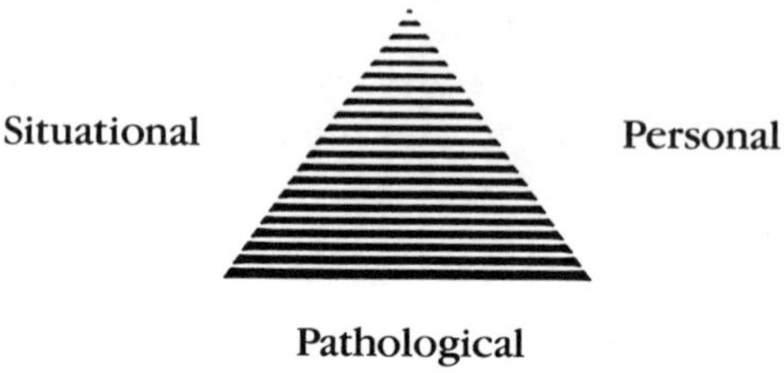

Regardless of the assessment tools utilized, your focus is on problem identification. Not only must you learn what the problems are, but also their depth and scope. Each of these factors will have a major impact on the plan and course of treatment. Some problems resist classification, but most can be categorized in terms of their level of severity.

Level I—Situational Problems

Most problems encountered in therapy result from situational difficulties. These problems fall within the framework of normal day-to-day stresses that all people encounter. This is not to say that Level I problems are not serious, just that they are common to the human experience. As a rule, these problems can be addressed through brief and nonintrusive intervention methods. A physical analogy to Situational Problems would be a cold or sinus infection. Examples of Level I (Situational Problems) include:

1. Relationship difficulties
2. Adjustment to death, divorce, or other trauma
3. Career or job conflicts
4. Role confusion
5. Minor behavior problems
6. Health issues
7. Transient stress reactions
8. Financial problems
9. Value conflict
10. Self-image problems

Level II —Personal Problems

When problems move outside of the range of usual human experience, they take on personal overtones. Personal problems are powerful and disruptive in that they impact on the emotional fabric of a person. At this level you see serious pain and discomfort, but there is a continued ability to function. The inner person is in distress but is not overwhelmed by the stresses of intrusive psychological forces. Because Level II problems are more pervasive, intervention methods and time factors are affected as well. Typically, personal problems run deeper than here-and-now adjustment concerns, and are flavored by unresolved past issues or future fears. An analogy of a physical cousin to a personal problem would be the flu or a case of measles. Examples of Level II problems include:

1. Recurring depression
2. Anxiety, panic attacks and phobic disorders
3. Substance abuse (mild to moderate)
4. Chronic relationship problems
5. Psychosomatic disorders
6. Antisocial behavior problems
7. Chronic employment problems
8. Identity confusion
9. Suicidal ideation
10. Sexual dysfunction

Level III — Pathological Problems

Pathological problems are the most serious and dysfunctional problems a person can encounter. These problems are not only damaging to the individual, but usually to those in proximity as well. Level III problems are indicative of major structural and foundation flaws within the individual. This does not mean that the person is bad, just that their psychological condition is painfully disrupted. Treatment will usually take longer periods of time and require greater intensity of intervention than with other levels. Cancer or diabetes can serve as a physical analogy to pathological problems. Examples of Level III problems include:

1. Sociopathic disorders
2. Schizophrenic disorders

3. Sexual abuse behaviors
4. Self-destructive and suicidal acts
5. Organic brain dysfunction
6. Chronic substance abuse
7. Paranoid disorders
8. Borderline disorders
9. Schizoid conditions
10. Chronic depressive disorders

Identifying the problem levels you are facing lays the groundwork for your intervention efforts. There is nothing wrong with labeling a person as long as the judgments you are making are flexible, nonrejecting, and subject to change. It is not uncommon for some helping professionals to confuse diagnosing a problem with treating the problem (Barten, 1971). The first is an accomplishment of value, but only as a means to the end of successful treatment.

CHAPTER 4

TREATING THE INDIVIDUAL

INTRODUCTION

People all think, feel, and do. They may not manifest these parts of themselves in the same manner or with the same depth, but all three are working from within. This trilogy is at the core of **IntraActive Therapy**. The therapist's therapeutic goal is to address the thinking, feeling, and doing part of the individual in a way that creates focus, balance, and resolution. These forces are not fixed. They change from day to day and even moment to moment. Generally, patterns emerge that can speak of a normal balance of the thinking, feeling, and doing self, or an imbalance that causes dysfunction. For some, the pattern may have the thinking self serving a dominant or misguided role. For others, the feeling or doing self may be the source of problems. With most people, problems that lead to therapy will involve all three forces.

TO THINK

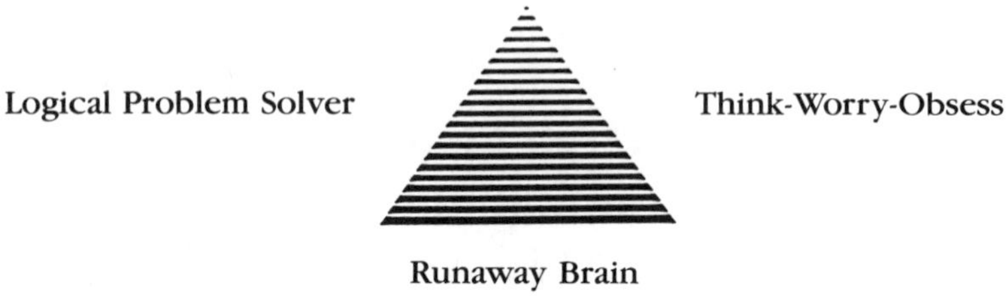

The Logical Problem Solver

The thinking part of people uses logic and reasoning to address life's problems. The mind helps in understanding and coping at a sophisticated level. Without the capacity to think, people would be limited to reactive and instinctive living. As it is, they are able to function in an independent and creative manner that exceeds that of all other living creatures.

Yet a mind, like everything in nature, must be kept in balance to best meet needs. If a mind is not used and trained, then the level of functioning is seriously limited. If a mind becomes dominant over other inner forces, then people become myopic in focus and restricted in their capacity to enjoy and experience life (Beck, 1967).

It takes a great deal of time, care, and energy to properly develop a mind. Although the time factor is not as crucial, care and energy are also necessary to repair a damaged or neglected mind. That is one of the marvelous attributes about the thinking part of a person, in that whatever is learned can be unlearned. It is possible to reverse old thinking patterns and to channel the mind on to a more effective level.

The thinking self is no more or less important than any other part of a person. The ability to think is an asset. The knowledge of how to think is a skill that is learned. If that learning has not occurred sufficient to an individual's needs, coping problems will develop. It is often the task of the therapist to initiate and facilitate thinking skills.

Think-Worry-Obsess

Thinking in the form of rational problem solving is constructive and positive. With constructive attention, most day-to-day personal problems can be solved with a few minutes of thought. Thinking that continues beyond a reasonable period of time takes the mind to other levels of utilization such as worry and obsession. When people move from thinking to worry and beyond, the balance discussed earlier is lost.

Worry is where people think about things beyond the point of trying to work them through. The mind continues to turn much like a washing machine agitator. It goes back and forth and never really goes anywhere. What is accomplished is to throw the mind further out of balance.

Worry feeds on itself. The more people worry, the more they tend to worry, and in this sense worry can be very addictive. Worry also blinds. People cannot think constructively if their minds are caught up in worry, so they miss much of what is going on. What they do see tends to be negative. As worries will mostly be bad, then the mind becomes increasingly sensitized to the negative. As worry and thinking grow increasingly negative, so do moods and attitudes. Worry is a harmful misuse of the thinking self.

When people worry extensively about one thing, they are becoming obsessive. Obsessive thinking has all of the drawbacks of worry increased tenfold. People become even more blind, negative, and dysfunctional (Polansky, 1971). The deeper the obsession, the more a mind controls instead of being controlled.

Pulling the thinking self away from worry and obsession is not easy. These tendencies are highly addictive, and the fight for control can be trying. A mind is like a nuclear power plant. When contained, managed, and channeled, it can do wondrous things. Left unchecked, it can self-destruct.

Runaway Brain

Sometimes when a mind is given too much control, it hijacks the ship. Worry and obsession lead to a condition called runaway brain. A mind runs free and it runs all the time. It may be thinking about important things, but not necessarily, and certainly the thinking that occurs is not productive. If you have ever seen a hamster running on an exercise wheel then you have an image of a runaway brain.

People who cannot sleep at night because their minds drift, or who wake up and immediately start thinking, are exhibiting symptoms of a runaway mind. Excessive daydreaming and fantasizing can also be indicators. If the primary reaction to stress is obsessive thinking, then it is likely that the mind has too much control.

When the thinking part of people gets out of balance, this not only limits the capacity to feel and do, but it can also self-destruct. The mind can turn so fast that it spins off track and shuts down. This can be a frightening experience that can substantially undermine functioning. Most people who have "nervous breakdowns" are experiencing a similar scenario.

The therapeutic task is to help the client bring his mind under control. Once this is achieved, your goal is to insure future balance and stability that keeps the thinking self as a functional asset versus destructive liability.

Primary Sources of Harm to the Thinking Self

1. Our Western culture overemphasizes the thinking self. This model can encourage overuse.
2. Thinking is concrete, understandable, and easy. It is natural to over rely on thinking as a primary coping resource.
3. The mind is powerful. Through imagination and fantasy, people can address problems that they otherwise feel ill equipped to handle. This process may help them actually avoid their realities if overused.
4. If the feeling or doing part of people is damaged, they will often try to overcompensate by magnifying the thinking self.
5. The thinking part of people has a great capacity for rationalization, denial, avoidance and other forms of self-protection. Consequently, they are more likely to view this part of themselves as an ally which they may over utilize.

TO FEEL

The feeling part of people senses and experiences. It does not take conscious effort or thought to feel, as most feelings occur in response to an individual's internal and external world. People have little direct control over their feelings, and feelings sometimes seem to have a mind of their own. Though feelings are divided into good/bad categories, all feelings serve positive functions that help in day-to-day living. It is said that man's capacity to think is what sets him apart from other living creatures. Actually it is the capacity to feel that is unique.

Their Nature—Our Friends

Feelings are our friends. They may not always feel good, but emotions offer powerful and special support. Feelings are more than random responses to stimulation. They serve as teachers and messengers in that they can guide toward an effective lifestyle. Some emotions like joy and serenity, can tell people that they are probably coping with life in an effective manner. Others like anxiety and depression, may be telling them the opposite. Either way, these feelings are serving in a positive fashion. The mind is one source of wisdom, but so too is the feeling self. It can sense things that the mind cannot pick up. Feelings are always communicating. Through their unique way of gaining attention, they have a special capacity to enlighten and guide.

Feelings also serve as a shock absorber between people and life. They take the impact of some of the harsher experiences and contain them in a way that enables a person to take the shock. Feelings may be intense, but they are gradual, helping to smooth out some of life's intrusions.

Pleasant and Unpleasant

Feelings are neither good nor bad, right or wrong—they simply are. When people think in terms of "good" and "bad," they naturally set up lists of emotions to pursue and emotions to avoid. In doing so, they may be stifling messengers of value. A better way to evaluate feelings is from a pleasant and unpleasant perspective. No one would argue that depression is a nice feeling, but it certainly can be a useful one. Depression may be a way for the feeling self to communicate that something is not right and that another look at lifestyle and necessary adjustments may be necessary. Without those unpleasant feelings of depression, mistakes might never be recognized. When feelings are viewed as good and bad, people try to set up filters to remove the bad and keep the good. They may not realize that these emotional filters are not selective, however. As undesired emotions are filtered out, they also find that the more desired ones are removed. Consequently, they end up feeling empty, numb, or dead—not "good." If feelings are polarized into "good" and "bad," then how do people feel about themselves when they have lots of bad feelings? "I feel bad a lot, therefore, I must be bad." People are also more vulnerable to ineffective coping methods as they always seek to feel good and to escape feeling bad.

Mishandled Feelings

Feeling parts of human nature cannot be thrown away. Try to bury them, run from them, or kill them, and emotions always seem to come back. If feelings could be discarded, most people would probably do a good bit of emotional house cleaning. It would be done to their detriment, however, as they would lose these valuable teachers.

Often the goal in life is to feel good. Feeling good is not the same thing as being good. There are things like drugs, money, power, and other distractions that can help people temporarily feel good when things may not actually be that good. Just because people feel good does not mean that they are effectively handling their emotions.

Many of the common emotional disorders encountered result from repressed emotion. Depression, panic attacks, phobias, and obsessive-compulsive disorders typically have a foundation of unaddressed emotion. Because emotions do not die of their own accord, they can unconsciously accumulate to overwhelming levels. The resulting pain distorts thinking and behavior and manifests itself in more serious psychological disorders.

The feeling part of everyone is where the sensitivity and capacity for love and enjoyment originate. When this part is killed, people become less effective with others, losing their ability to enjoy and experience life. They may continue to exist but they will not thrive. There is a decided difference between surviving and living.

The emotional part of people is every bit as important as the thinking and doing parts. Unfortunately, because it is also the source of pain, the emotional self is the part most quickly shunned and neglected. For many clients, healing the feeling self and bringing it back on line will be the major therapeutic agenda (Rabkin, 1977).

Primary Sources of Harm to the Feeling Self

1. If life carries more pain than can be handled, the feeling self shuts down. This happens most often in early childhood.
2. When unpleasant feelings occur, even though caused by others, people tend to blame themselves and repress their emotions. Others may be the source of the pain, but people feel that hurt within and resent themselves for it.

3. Children feel naturally. If their adult models mishandle their feelings, children unlearn that natural feeling ability and replicate these adult examples.
4. Because feelings can be very unpleasant, people may come to view this part of themselves as an enemy. By resenting the emotional self, they are really rejecting themselves.
5. Feelings are powerful but intangible. People tend to reject things that cannot be easily defined or understood.

TO DO

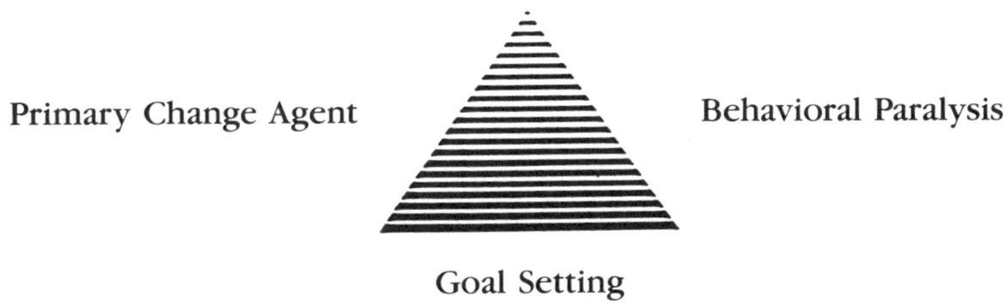

The doing self brings it all together. It translates the thinking and feeling parts into action. People can feel or think anyway they choose, but what they do will be the bottom line on which they succeed or fail. Although doing is a by-product of thinking and feeling, doing also helps determine how people think and feel. It is the most tangible resource for growth and change.

The Primary Change Agent

The doing part of people is the most visible and measurable component. When they do, they are producing the results of thought and feeling and translating both into behavior. Because behavior is visible and measurable, doing is risky. Actions may produce positive results, or bring failure and ridicule.

Just as the doing part can impact on the outside world, there is also great influence on the inner self. What people do has a powerful impact on what they feel and think (Fagan and Shepherd, 1970). If they change what they do, they will eventually change how they feel and think. The transition is gradual but dynamic.

There is hope in the power of the doing self. In that people and others can see their actions, they then have something concrete to work on. In contrast, trying to change feelings is much harder because feelings are so intangible. If it is true that actions change emotions, then feelings can be indirectly altered by directing behavior. Change can be generated in something hard to understand by altering something easy to understand.

Behavior is the therapist's single greatest change agent. By helping clients channel their actions you can dramatically alter their interface with their world and their inner selves. It is exciting, because focusing on changing behavior is a solid activity that even the most dysfunctional individual can undertake (Phillips and Wiener, 1966). Changing one little behavior today moves clients toward the larger potential target behaviors of tomorrow. The process is progressive and positive when you look at behavior in terms of what works and does not work as compared to what is right and what is wrong.

If the behavior is changed the feelings will follow. Everyone has had the experience of fearing something, doing it anyway, and finding the fear subsiding. Days could have been spent just telling the feeling to leave. Actions have the power to make it happen when words do not.

Behavioral Paralysis

When people are raised in a world that is critical, they naturally come to fear any action that can lead to further hurt. Since essentially anything done has this potential, many become behaviorally paralyzed. If they act, then they are at risk. Therefore, they do not act.

Behavioral paralysis can run the gamut from mild inhibition to total dysfunction. Agoraphobia is an example of behavioral paralysis in an extreme form. Not calling for a date because of fear of rejection or avoidance of talking in groups are examples of milder behavioral paralysis.

This concept is important not only because of the impact it has on interfacing with the world, but also its effect on feelings and thoughts. Behavioral paralysis leads to paralysis at the feeling and thinking levels as well. People who begin to shut down behaviorally soon begin to feel and think differently. This reaction leads to further inhibition of behavior and so forth. The outcome is a vicious circle that leads to a progressive loss of functioning.

In most therapeutic situations, effort will need to be directed toward breaking the cycle of behavioral paralysis. Facilitating activity and movement around problem issues will liberate the total person. Doing people are generally more healthy than less active people, and less prone to overpowering emotional problems. Your therapeutic task is to help clients begin moving forward and to upgrade their level of doing.

Goal Setting

Changing behavior is difficult. In making this effort, patterns that have an entrenched history are altered. Generally, the more purposeful and directed the changes, the better the potential for success. Goals provide such a basis for change (Sifneos, 1972).

Goals are destinations that people set for themselves. Any trip is more likely to be successful if people have a clear view of where they are heading. Thus, goals set the path toward change. By targeting the doing self, people can gradually shift old patterns to new more effective ones. Goals make the trip a bit easier by pulling people forward. Without the direction of goals, the energy investment will not produce matching achievement.

When people quit their efforts toward growth, they begin their movement toward death. In consequence, defining and setting goals is important not only to those in therapy, but to everyone who wants to keep life moving in a healthy direction. Goals are much like a program for a computer. No matter how powerful the hardware, without a program it is a limited resource. A program provides focus and definition that maximizes the computer's power.

Most people who seek therapy already operate from a set of goals. Problems arise when these goals are unconscious, maladaptive, or destructive. Their whole basis for living may stem from a need to punish others who have caused hurt. Being unaware of this goal, people can live through anger and vengeance unknowingly, but certainly to their detriment. One of the primary thrusts of therapy is to pull life goals into the open, make necessary alterations, and then facilitate movement toward these new directions.

Primary Sources of Harm to the Doing Self

1. Doing represents skill. If people have not been shown or taught how to do, then they do not develop doing skills.
2. The more people do, the more they are able to do. Conversely, the less people do, the less they are able to do.

3. Doing involves risk. Without an encouraging and positive support system, this risk can seem overwhelming. Therefore, people do not act.
4. Feelings and thought should influence, not determine actions. Sometimes people have to do without the backup of the emotional or thinking self or be paralyzed.
5. People live in a perfectionistic world. If they cannot be certain of success, they fear to try, and thus, fail to learn and grow in their capacity to do.

THINKING INTERVENTIONS

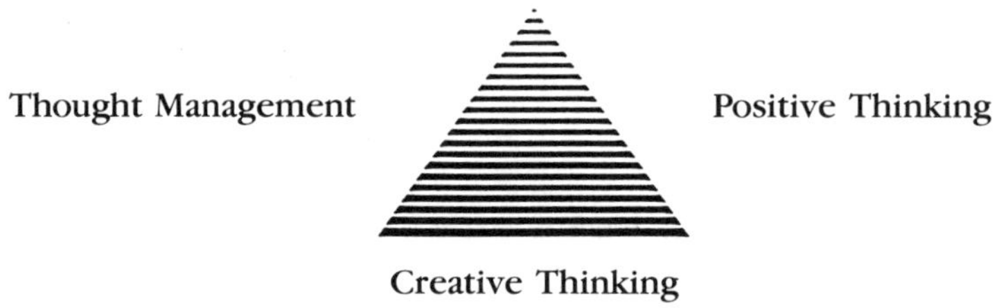

When the thinking part of a person gets out of control, it takes over. The mind demands energy and time and runs continually. It takes over when it wants to. A person wakes up thinking and goes to bed thinking. The mind turns throughout the day unless distracted by an external force. The more out of control the mind is, the stronger that distraction must become. It is typical to seek the relief provided by alcohol and drugs which temporarily slow down the thinking self. What the mind thinks about can be very important or very trivial. In any case, it continues to turn and process like a computer, searching for answers to unsolvable questions. A runaway mind is exhausting.

Thought Management and Redirection

When the thinking self gets out of balance, it is important that individuals have some sense of their capacity to regain control (Wolpe, 1990). One concrete technique is called thought management or thought control. There is no magic in this technique. You simply instruct clients to begin saying NO or STOP when their minds start to drift or move toward worry and obsession. In doing so, they enter into battle for their own mind that can be a difficult tug of war. Some people have to say NO a hundred times a day, but persistency brings control.

At first, when the mind is told NO or STOP it may not back down for more than a few seconds. By fighting back, this time increases to where the mind activates on command rather than on it is own. In more extreme cases, this struggle can take weeks. Thought management will not always work by itself. It may be one of ten conjunctive methods clients will use to regain control of their thinking selves. For many people, however, it is a simple and workable technique that they can put to immediate practical use.

One of the most common sources of a dominant thinking self is misuse of the mind. Thinking patterns can encourage a misbalance. For example, by responding to problems with obsessive thinking, people are training the mind to react in this fashion. When they spend a great deal of time fantasizing and dreaming, they are teaching their minds to take control. Later when they feel that things are a bit out of hand, it may be too late to just shut it off. The mind has been spoiled to the extent that it is used to having control and they will have to work to regain command.

Thought redirection is a technique to be used preventively as well as after the fact. This approach to disciplining the mind centers on keeping mental energies generally aimed in a purposeful and productive direction. Much like disciplining a child, clients set the standards for their thinking and direct their thinking toward those standards. There is certainly nothing wrong with occasionally letting the mind drift, worry, or the like, but these times should be the exception not the rule. By keeping the mind channeled it is kept under control.

Positive Thinking

No matter where people are, they will find the existence of good and bad. Because the bad is what can cause the greatest discomfort, it is natural that their minds would focus in this direction. As this occurs, they can become addicted to negative thinking while losing the capacity to see the positive. A pattern of negative thinking can develop that influences feelings and actions. People think negatively and begin to feel and behave the same way (Carnigie, 1936). As a consequence, it is important that they keep their minds focused in a more positive direction.

Many people have what I call "a big eye on the bad stuff and a little eye on the good stuff." Your task is to help clients reverse this emphasis. A simple technique for beginning this change is to follow the "three to one" rule. For every negative topic clients think about, they should make sure that they notice three positives. One to one the negative has more power; two to one and the positive and negative neutralize one another; three to one creates a more positive mind-set.

Positive thinking does not mean that people must artificially create the good and ignore the bad. The good is there; they may not be used to seeing it. The bad is there, too. They must train their minds to see it, respond as appropriate, and then let it go and move on to the good. It is the obsessing, waiting for, and lingering around the bad stuff of life that gets people into trouble.

Within everyone is a little voice. That little voice can be an ally or an enemy. If it constantly criticizes and attacks, then clearly it is the latter. That little voice is created and programmed in youth. Lots of love, support, and direction on the outside create a positive little voice on the inside. Anything less, and the voice becomes a critic. No matter what the emphasis of the little voice, it can be retrained. By ignoring, turning off, or even getting a little mad at the little voice when it is being negative, people can begin to turn things around. Pushing that little voice to be encouraging, positive, and constructive can carry the program the rest of the way. A positive little voice becomes a friend that can be carried throughout life.

Creative Thinking

I believe it is almost impossible to be creative and depressed at the same time. There is something about creating that takes people beyond their inner selves and places them on a higher plane of functioning (May, 1975). Creativity may include painting, writing, or another art form. Yet more often than not, the best creative outlets will be day-to-day real-life involvements. There is always opportunity to find ways to do what people do better. There are plenty of chances to increase efficiency and expand horizons. In doing so, people shift their focus from internal to external issues. That transition is important if the mind tends to be too self-focused.

Like much of human experience, creativity is more a learned skill than an inherited ability. It is something that must be worked at. Most people feel they lack creative ability and as a result settle for reactive behaviors. This is one of the reasons there are more followers than leaders. Yet creativity is a crucial ingredient in problem solving, personal growth, relationship development, and maturation in general. It is a skill that cannot be neglected (Adler, 1956).

By therapeutically stimulating clients toward creative thinking, you help expand their capacity to maximally benefit from and channel their thinking selves. Rather than a mind that reacts, worries, and agitates about the external world, through creativity the mind becomes a constructive and supportive tool for successful living.

How do people create? They start looking for little ways to do things more effectively. They intentionally explore alternatives and take chances by implementing the better ones. Mistakes are a part of creativity. Remember your first artistic effort? With time and persistency, successes tend to exceed creative failures. Imagine the strong impact on self-confidence and personal effectiveness that creativity of the mind can bring.

FEELING INTERVENTIONS

Sensitization

Free Feeling

Emotional Catharsis

Changing the way a client handles feelings is probably the most difficult intervention you will attempt. Our culture maximizes the thinking and doing self and tends to minimize the feeling self. That is not to say that feeling good is not on the list, just that emotions in general are more taboo than thinking and doing. By now you know, however, that this part of everyone is as significant as the others. It is important to have the emotional self fully functional and free.

Sensitization

This intervention method involves an awakening of the feeling self. You will find that many clients feel emotionally numb or dead. They can feel some emotions intensely for brief periods, but generally their emotional selves have shut down. Most of what they do feel will be depression, anguish, or anger. As a consequence, they feel victimized by their emotional selves and try even harder to turn this part off.

Most people turn off their emotional faucet during their youth, a period when they are most vulnerable to emotional pain and least able to understand and handle it. No matter how hard they turn the handle, a little bit of emotion will continue to leak out into their consciousness. Unfortunately, what leaks out is generally unpleasant. Their interpretation is that those leaks represent most of what is stored in the tank, and so they try hard to keep the lid on tight. In doing so, they inhibit their ability to enjoy life fully, thereby stifling a crucial part of their personhood.

Sensitization is nothing more than turning the faucet back on. The therapist's goal is to facilitate a gradual reacquaintance of client with his emotional self. This is accomplished by:

1. Encouraging the person to seek opportunities to feel (pleasant or unpleasant) and to let those feelings come out.
2. Educating the client to the importance of the feeling self and trying to transfer the idea of bringing this part back to life.
3. Providing a supportive and nurturing opportunity for the person to face his emotional self without fear of judgment, rejection, or desertion.

Sensitization serves to unblock and activate emotions. Once people see that they can feel, and that their feelings do not destroy them, they are more able to recognize the benefits of having the emotional self alive and well and open for business.

Free Feeling

One of Sigmund Freud's analytical techniques was called free association (Kline, 1972). Basically the patient was encouraged to let the mind roam free and to share whatever thoughts came into consciousness. Free feeling is much the same thing, but it addresses the emotional self.

Free feelings first require that clients shut down their minds through practiced thought stoppage, and then allow their feelings to come out. No effort is made to analyze or judge the emotions that arise, and they are allowed to flow through the inner self unrestricted. When clients are able to do so, the body of their emotions becomes defused and flows away.

This process can be frightening. If clients have a reservoir of painful emotion, and it starts emptying, they can easily believe they are going to drown in their emotions. This is not possible. People cannot hold enough feelings to destroy themselves. Just as you cannot fill a cup with enough water to break it, people cannot hold enough pain to break them. There is one exception to consider, though. If a lid is put on that cup and it is placed in the freezer, the water can expand and break the cup. Similarly, if emotions are contained and thought to death, people can expand the power of emotions to an overwhelming degree.

Practicing free feeling will not make all emotions go away. Depending on how much is inside, a good bit will go back to the container. Every time free feeling is practiced, however, a measure of old emotion will be released, gradually cleaning out the reservoir. If clients can do that, then their emotional selves become less intimidating and harmful (Rabkin, 1977).

Free feeling is best accomplished when individuals are alone and with minimal distractions. The effort is to let whatever is in there come out and be felt. The more it is felt, the more it is released. In doing so, clients discover that even painful emotions are bearable if they give them free rein. They flow through like electricity, and then go elsewhere. Much of the pain of unpleasant emotions comes from the restrictions created for those feelings.

Free feeling is a source of emotional exercise. The more emotions are allowed to come out, the stronger the emotional self becomes in its capacity to support.

Emotional Catharsis

Emotional trauma can produce powerful emotional residue. Abuse as a child, combat, death of a loved one, major illness, and other difficult experiences can leave emotions that are not easily dislodged. Sometimes it is necessary to produce a cathartic reaction in order to defuse these emotions.

Catharsis is serious, but not generally dangerous. Contrary to myth, stirring up major emotions will not push a person off the deep end (Griest et al., 1986). If mishandled, such actions will create further pain and inhibition, but rarely more than that.

You can therapeutically facilitate catharsis through the following process:

1. Explore the source and nature of the emotional experience as much as possible.
2. Provide a quiet and supportive setting for the client and establish a clear goal of addressing the emotionally charged issue.
3. Through visual imagery, role playing, or verbal exploration stimulate thought and emotion around the cathartic issue.

4. Encourage spontaneous emotional release in whatever form it may take. Help the person let it out, show it, and face it with full force and power.
5. Having experienced the depth of their feeling, allow the clients opportunity to recover and recount their experience. Endorse their effort and reinforce their conclusions and resolution efforts.

Through emotional catharsis the therapist is able to jar loose emotional roadblocks that can undermine other therapeutic efforts. Repeated attempts may be necessary to free up entrenched and pervasive emotion, but no emotional trauma is permanent. With persistency, old emotion can be dislodged.

CHAPTER 5

INTERVENTION METHODS

INTRODUCTION

As a short-term therapist, you have many frameworks from which you can initiate intervention. All have strengths and weaknesses, and most treatment efforts will incorporate multiple treatment methods.

THE PRIMARY TREATMENT MODALITIES

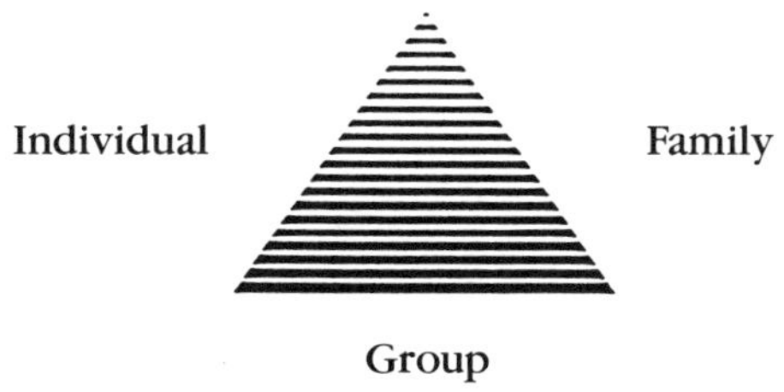

Individual Therapy

One-on-one therapy is the path that most therapists take toward intervention. Many clients acquaint therapy with this approach and most interventions at least begin with individual therapy.

Advantages

1. Individual focus
2. Nonthreatening
3. Flexible

4. Insurance reimbursable
5. Conducive to intimacy

Disadvantages

1. Expensive
2. Sometimes lacks real-world context
3. Limited quality control
4. Insulated exposure
5. Availability and time limitations

Family Therapy

Family involvement can serve as a dynamic source of insight and change. The family system can be the cause of emotional dysfunction, but also a source of insight and resolution (Bowen, 1978).

Advantages

1. Excellent historical information resource
2. Powerful and cathartic influence
3. Foundation support system
4. Source of primary models
5. Cost and resource efficient

Disadvantages

1. Threatening and intrusive to some clients
2. Scheduling difficulties
3. Complicates relationship variables
4. Seldom reimbursed under insurance
5. Mixed participant agendas

Group Therapy

Groups provide diverse and practical help. They offer distinct advantages that have application to most therapeutic situations.

Advantages

1. Provides diverse exposure
2. Offers unique support opportunities
3. Very cost efficient
4. Has a stronger real world context
5. Can be targeted to specific needs

Disadvantages

1. Can be very threatening
2. Not suitable to some conditions
3. May lack personalization
4. May not suffice as a stand alone therapy
5. High issue avoidance potential

A combination of these treatment approaches would be considered ideal in facilitating short-term intervention. Multifaceted treatment intervention helps compensate for drawbacks in singular intervention, and in maintaining a more dynamic emphasis on change and resolution.

SECONDARY INTERVENTIONS

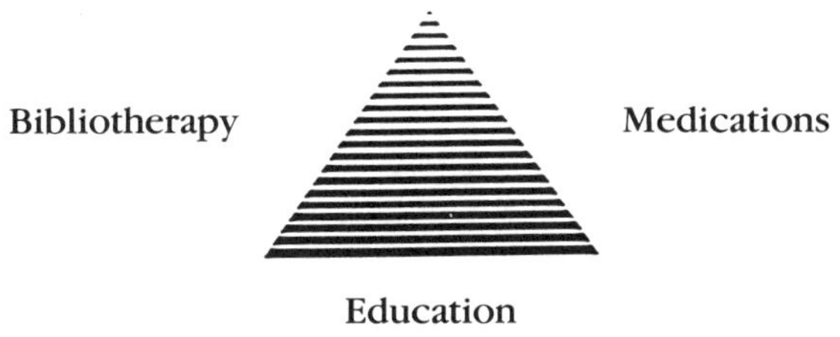

These interventions serve as supplemental supports to the primary intervention modalities. In most cases they should not stand alone, but they can have necessary and beneficial impact on the treatment outcome.

Bibliotherapy

Reading can provide insights and directions that are not available elsewhere, and do so in a comfortable and convenient fashion. Almost everyone in therapy should consider reading as an important resource. (See Appendix.)

Advantages

1. Inexpensive
2. Accessible
3. Nonthreatening
4. Information intensive
5. Easily targeted to need

Disadvantages

1. Exaggerated expectations
2. Lacks relationship variable
3. Minimally personalized
4. Interpretation problems
5. Conflictual information

Medications

Medications are not a magical answer to the psychological problems of our culture (Allport, 1968). Certainly, it can be effectively argued that that there are a number of situations where medications are a treatment of choice (Ayd, 1975). However, your efforts here are to address mainstream problems, and most common disorders respond better to medication as a supplemental part of the therapeutic process (Lewis, 1991). Prescribing, by law, is left to those who are trained and licensed to medicate. If you have this license, take care not to neglect your other avenues for change. If you prescribe, keep a positive eye toward medications as a helping resource and make an effort to have a working knowledge of the various contributions medications can make.

Advantages

1. Convenient and broadly available
2. Cost efficient
3. Can be targeted to individual need
4. Can reduce symptoms and allow other interventions
5. Critical to the management of some conditions

Disadvantages

1. Encourage abrogation of personal responsibility
2. Facilitate external dependencies
3. Provide symptom relief versus problem relief
4. Side effects
5. Suicide and overdose potential

Education

Seminars, courses, and other educational opportunities are major resources for growth and change. Education serves a major role in mental health, and should be a part of almost all treatment situations (Glasser, 1965).

Advantages

1. Cost effective
2. Nonthreatening
3. Can be personalized
4. Culturally acceptable
5. Diverse resource availability

Disadvantages

1. Limited quality control
2. Practicality may not be emphasized
3. Lack of aftercare or follow-up
4. Minimal personalization
5. Resources can be difficult to find

Each of these primary and secondary treatment approaches has unique facets that can facilitate short-term intervention. Effective treatment is much like cross-training in athletics. Multifaceted training enhances an athlete's performance in his specific sport beyond the level that singular training can provide. The cross-training concept has equal application to short-term therapy.

CHAPTER 6

KEYS TO SUCCESSFUL SHORT-TERM INTERVENTION

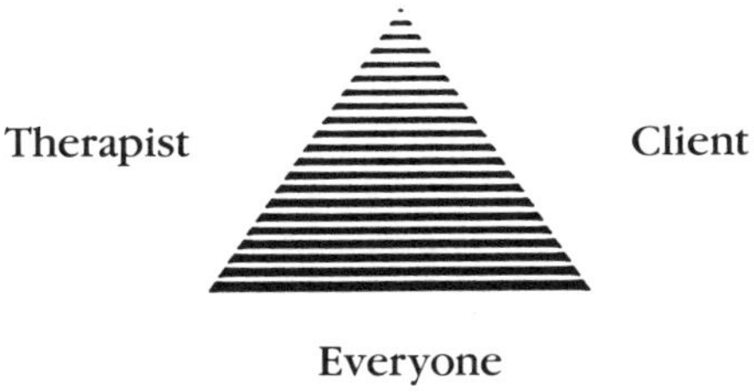

INTRODUCTION

Short-term therapy is a specific and intentional therapeutic approach, and there are certain areas of emphasis that help make short-term therapy effective. Some of these components involve the therapist, some the client, and some both, but all play a part in an effective therapeutic relationship.

THE THERAPIST

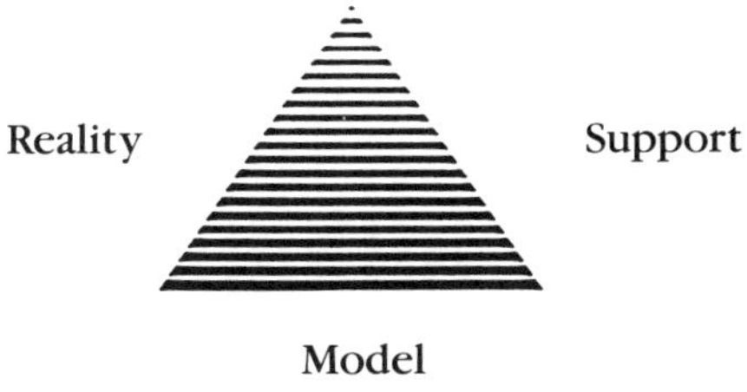

The therapist is the leader of the therapeutic process. Client-centered therapy does not mean client-directed therapy. People enter into therapy seeking insights and answers that they cannot discover for themselves. The therapist's role is to provide direction beyond what a person can find elsewhere. This contribution can be best presented through your focus on reality, your support, and your model.

Reality

Good therapy helps people handle the real world. Creating an artificial therapeutic environment limits the long-term outcome for the client. The real world holds people accountable and makes them responsible for their own lives. The real world is confrontive and demands effort and energy. There is little patience in the real world for those who hide, avoid, or live in fantasy. An effective therapist is one who helps people to recognize, understand, and face their realities (Glasser, 1965).

A reality focus requires candor, a willingness to confront, and practicality. **Candor** is important in that most people have a hard time finding people who will tell them the truth. In an effort to avoid conflict or hurting feelings, people will distort the truth and give an artificial feedback. A candid and courageous therapist will give a mirror image of reality, not a confusing or misleading fun house image (Bergman, 1985).

Confrontation is not the same as an attack. When therapists confront they are sharing reality in a direct and straightforward manner. The goal of confrontation is to reach the individual, not abuse him. This type of direct communication is necessary, but rare in our culture (Loew et al., 1975). It is surprising how direct confrontation can open eyes to realities that may not otherwise be recognized.

There are many therapeutic techniques, but the ones you use most should have a strong measure of attached **practicality** (Allport, 1968). Practical interactions teach about real life and prepare clients for dealing with reality. A practical emphasis is especially important in short-term therapy due to the time and resource limitations. Therapy that is practical will have meaningful and long standing results.

Support

In child rearing, the parents who love but fail to discipline will damage their child. Conversely, the parent who disciplines but fails to love will also do harm. An emphasis on both is necessary and this is also true of short-term therapy. Candor, confrontation, and practicality must be balanced by support. This support is represented by your efforts to **care**, offer **sensitivity** and give **attention**.

I am not sure that successful therapy is possible without caring, sensitivity and attention from the therapist. In fact, this support may be the most crucial element of a therapeutic relationship (Wolpe, 1990). People respond better when they feel genuine concern.

It is easy to see how this process works. Nearly everyone needs affection and acceptance. Much of peoples' lives are spent searching for fulfillment of these needs (Moustakas, 1974). Yet unconditional acceptance and support are rare in our culture. When people find it, and believe it is genuine, they hold on to it.

A balanced emphasis on reality and support will do more for your clients than any other effort you can make on their behalf. This concern has to be real. As a therapist, you will have to commit yourself to clients in a way that keeps your feelings on a positive and loving level. You can only fake it so far.

Showing your support may come in the form of check-up calls following a visit, hugs, praise, or being available for crisis calls. Whatever the method, your support should offer help, not harm, and will, more than any other factor, determine the treatment outcome.

Model

What people say has a great deal of power. What they do has even more. This is especially true for a therapist as clients come to you for insight and answers. They are looking for solutions and you can bet they pay close attention to the examples you set (Bandura, 1965).

Your model is important from several perspectives. It plays an important part in **clients' acceptance** of you. If they find your model distasteful, ineffective, or eccentric, they are less likely to engage in a legitimate therapeutic process.

Your model also establishes your **credibility**. If you live your life in a way that seems reasonable and mature, they people have faith in your ability to help them get to that point. They will be more likely to follow your path if that path seems to work for you.

Many therapists do not believe in making the therapeutic relationship a personal one (Glasser, 1965). They believe that their lifestyles are not really any of their clients' business. That may be true, but like it or not, clients will make it their business. They are looking to you for help and they will want to know if you know how to make this business of living work. If you cannot run your own life, they will not have **faith** in your ability to help them run their own.

As therapists, you do not have to be perfect. It is important that you work to grow and reach your own potential. You probably cannot help a client reach any further in life than you can.

THE CLIENT

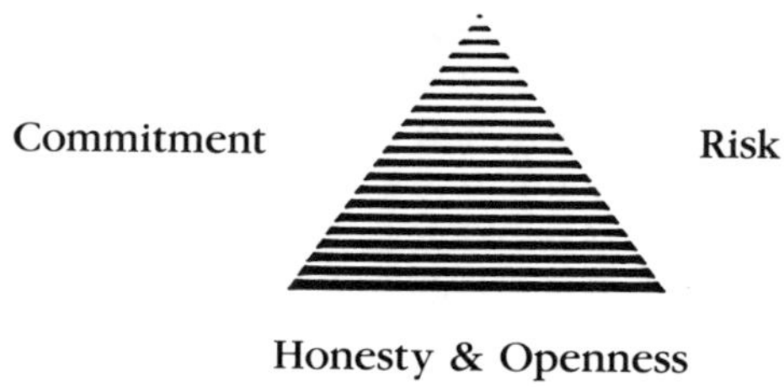

IntraActive short-term therapy is a partnership. The therapist must carry his or her end, but so too must clients be encouraged to share the burden. Commitment, risk, honesty, and openness are the clients' responsibility to the relationship.

Commitment

Therapy is hard. It can be painful, disruptive, expensive, and time consuming. Like any medicine, clients may have to endure a little bitterness to receive the benefits. Without a strong commitment, it is difficult to sustain active participation in therapy. That commitment should be centered on a willingness to **identify**, **explore**, and **address** personal issues. Such a commitment is easily stated, less easily maintained. Yet it is important in that all therapy has rough spots that require a measure of commitment for us to get through.

Commitment to a therapy process does not mean "anything goes." If clients feel that things are not progressing as they should or if they are otherwise dissatisfied, they should have the right to stop therapy. However, therapy should not be discontinued until they have talked through their concerns and made an effort to resolve them. If clients are going to quit, then they should be encouraged to do so in a mature and responsible fashion. That kind of commitment will prevent unnecessary therapeutic breakdowns.

Risk

Change requires risk. Moving from here to there represents some danger. It is not possible to be safe and in transition at the same moment. Since most clients are in some pain already, it is understandable that they would seek protection from further hurt. Therapy can mean safety instead of **change** for some people, and short-term therapy does not accept safety as an end unto itself.

Therapy is a process of **controlled** risk. The clients take chances that are preplanned and with the **backup** from you, the therapist. There is risk, but it is calculated risk that stacks the odds in the clients' favor. Clients will not be able to win unless they can find the willingness to play.

Honesty and Openness

By the time people leave childhood, most have learned to hide their inner selves. By adulthood, they have become accustomed to living behind a mask of illusion and dishonesty. They do not necessarily distort the truth, but they usually are practiced at hiding it.

Short-term therapy will not work without a good measure of honesty and openness. The clients have to let you know what they think, feel, and do for you to know how to lend your hand. Conceal significant information about any of these three forces, and they seriously limit the treatment outcome.

Honesty can be **encouraged** by example. As the therapist, you should avoid telling even the smallest falsehood to clients. If you are dishonest about one thing, then they will wonder what else you might have lied about. Your example can help ease them into the alien position of being honest and open about who they are and how they live.

To initiate change requires starting from a **reality**-based foundation. Truth represents that foundation. Honesty and openness provide a point for you and your clients to begin.

Honesty and openness are **progressive**. It feels good to be genuine and have nothing to hide. It saves a great deal of energy and frees you and your clients for other investments. The more clients are able to practice honesty and openness with you, the more they will want to. Honesty is addictive.

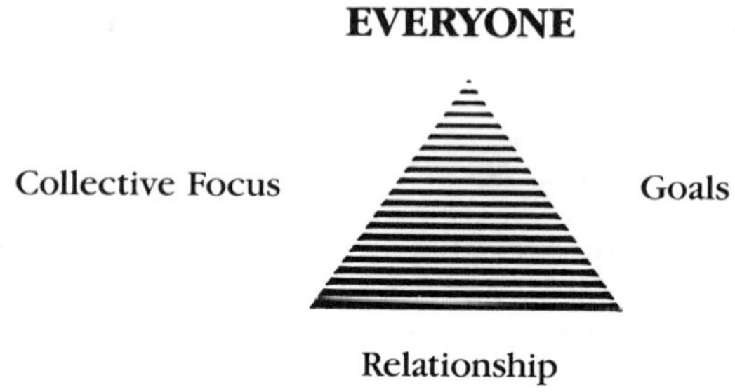

Short-term therapy is a cooperative effort requiring joint areas of emphasis from everyone involved. This partnership is a powerful foundation for change that involves collective focus, goals, and relationship.

Collective Focus

All therapy sessions should be productive, but some will be more productive than others. Generally, the stronger the focus, the greater that productivity will be. Three areas of emphasis that stand out are historical issues, psychological issues, and situational issues.

Historical issues are important not only in that they provide background information, but also in that they can be sources of unresolved pain or restraint. An unsettled past hinders people in their efforts to live their lives fully today and tomorrow. Many live their lives carrying a backpack in which they store the mistakes and bad experiences encountered on their journey. Both the therapist and client need to be alerted to the task of consistently reaching into the pack, exploring these historical issues that remain a burden, and finding ways to toss them away.

Certainly internal **psychological issues** are also an important part of the focus. Looking at the ways people think, do, and feel and trying to understand and make changes in these areas is all part of this process. Liberating the psychological self can be both exciting and frightening. Clients may be afraid of what they will find or of damaging themselves more, so they may try to avoid this area. Both the therapist and clients must press forward in their mutual efforts to understand and address the psychological self.

Historical and psychological issues are important, but so, too, are the daily **situational issues** encountered. The outside world is dynamic and presents us with a variety of situational concerns. It is legitimate for the therapist to help clients face situational problems. Like the missionary preaching to a starving man, you are not going to be heard until you help with the pressing issue of starvation. The clients' situation will often speak too loudly for them to focus on other important issues.

Most sessions should focus on historical, psychological, and situational issues. The measure of emphasis will vary from session to session, but all three are necessary focal points requiring energy from the therapist, client, and others who are actively involved.

Goals

Clients have to know where they are heading if they are to determine where they wind up. Goals provide direction that pull them toward growth. Goals help them frame how they choose to think, feel, and do in their efforts to change.

As a rule, the therapeutic process should include both **short- and long-term goals**. These goals should be developed by both client and therapist. Once the goals are defined, then comes commitment. The time for exploration and questioning should be before they commit, not after. It is hard enough at the beginning to reach personal growth goals; without strong commitment, it can be impossible. If clients are constantly doubting and resisting their goals, then they are not likely to reach them.

Generally, the client and therapist should each bring an agenda to a therapy session. **Agendas** help keep each session purposeful. It is also a good idea to review goals that have been established before. Review keeps goals alive and conscious.

It also helps to recognize goals that have been obtained. Certainly new goals should be established, but so too should **accomplishments** be recognized.

Reaching a goal lays the groundwork for a new goal. Crossing a mountain enables people to see the one beyond. Goals are magnets that pull clients along. They need that force as a guide and companion. Without it they are like a ship without a rudder, reaching its destination only through fate and chance.

Relationship

The client/therapist relationship should be an **intimate** one (Rogers, 1951). It should function within ethical boundaries, but also follow normal patterns of healthiness and maturity. Distance, cold professionalism, deception, and passivity do not meet these criteria.

The therapeutic relationship is a marriage of sorts. Each party should be **bonded** to the other. The effort should be to establish a level of closeness that facilitates client growth and change. A mechanical, detached, dishonest or dependent relationship is less conducive to this goal.

In a healthy marriage, problems are discussed openly and worked through. Each individual is **sensitive** to the needs of the other and relates in a fashion that keeps the level of intimacy alive and thriving. The client/therapist relationship is no different. Do what is best for one another, not what comes easily, conveniently, or without personal threat. The nature of the client/therapist relationship will determine the success of the therapeutic effort.

CHAPTER 7

THE THERAPEUTIC PROCESS

Beginning Phase

Intervention Phase

Resolution Phase

INTRODUCTION

Therapy is a process not an event. It occurs over time and involves points of transition and development. These phases can be specifically defined, but in reality they overlap with each session and ebb and flow over the course of treatment (Gustafson, 1986). Too, these phases represent the ideal. Each person's growth pattern will be different, and the absence or alteration of segments of these phases need not represent failure. Knowing the likely course of treatment, you can better channel the process and measure your movement toward resolution.

BEGINNING PHASE

Apprehension

Anyone who enters into therapy will be confused and uncertain. Clients will come with dated images and apprehensions typical to any new, and in this case, seemingly mystical experience. This apprehension can be a blessing in that the person is participating in a new experience and will likely be open to direction and structure. If unsupported, these same apprehensions can paralyze the client to a point of nonparticipation or withdrawal (Rank, 1945).

There are three keys to addressing clients' apprehensions in the beginning phase of therapy. First, your demonstration of **candor**, **openness**, and **genuine concern** will help alleviate many of their concerns. New experiences are more tolerable if clients go through them with a partner they can trust for support. That relationship can turn therapy from an act of anguish into an adventure.

Information on the ins and outs of therapy can also help ease apprehensions. Provide written information to the client before therapy and explain the details directly once they begin. Continue to explore the whats, whys, and hows throughout the therapeutic process. The more the clients know, the better they can address their apprehensions.

Lastly, demonstration of **expertise** can instill confidence in therapy. Let your clients know your experience, educational background, skills, and credentials. These things are no guarantee of your effectiveness, but they are a partial measurement of your qualifications to help.

Expectations

People begin therapy with many expectations. Depending on the exposure they have had, the clients' images may be **realistic or fantastical**.

The latter is more likely, especially in view of the historical (a serious, bearded, pipe-smoking older man studiously listening to the vague ramblings of the reclining patient) view of therapy and the Hollywood portrayals (sincere and wise therapist who works miracles with the disturbed and misunderstood client).

Again, clients' expectations can work for or against therapy. If their expectations are minimal or realistic, your good efforts will be appreciated and pursued. If, on the other hand, they come for miracles, their disappointment, unless countered, will undermine their involvement.

Unreasonable expectations can be countered with rational information. Some people will cling to magic no matter what you do, but most will respond to **common sense information** on what therapy should be like and most likely will be like for them (Allport, 1968).

Unreasonable expectations tend to fade for everyone over time. They cling to high expectations because they have a high need for relief. Disappointment may occur in the beginning when clients recognize there is no quick and easy fix. As they begin to gain a sense of their own power to grow and change, these expectations will be replaced with more reasonable hope.

Inconsistency

The beginning stages of therapy are characterized by client inconsistencies. They may miss appointments or come unprepared. Their interest in therapy may be strong at times and marginal at others. This initial inconsistency is **typical** of the early stages of therapy.

Therapy is not an easy undertaking. It requires a strong commitment of energy, time, and money. Unless and until clients become **fully attached** to treatment involvement, occasional flagging enthusiasm is to be expected.

You can best help by pointing out inconsistent involvement and encouraging the clients' good efforts. To you, practiced as you may be, therapy is easy to understand and the difficulty easy to take for granted. On the other end, someone who already has a good measure of pain and stress, may not view therapy with the same eye of enthusiasm. Your **support** and continued commitment to the person will best insure his or her consistent involvement.

INTERVENTION PHASE

The initial stages of short-term therapy can take as little as a few minutes and as much as three or four visits. By this time, if the relationship is jelling, the process should be moving into the intervention phase. This will be the time when you and the client will make your best strides toward resolution. If a therapeutic process is moving in a constructive direction, several variables will come into play. Elements of transition, dependency, and intention will characterize the process.

Transition

Growth brings change. Whenever people move from something that is known to something that is unknown, they go through an awkward period of transition. This phase is much like having one foot on one side of a creek bank and the other foot on the other side. They are not on either side and the position can be disconcerting. Their effort is to cross this creek and move to the better, albeit **unknown**, side.

The temporary **limbo** that results from transition is a time of doubt. Clients are treading waters that they have not experienced. The changes they are pursuing may be for the better, but they do not know that for sure. What they had before may have been bad, but it was familiar, and they know it was survivable. This uncertainty can breed ambivalence, the need for extra support, and resistance. All are transitional reactions to which the short-term therapist must give particular attention.

The therapist's role is to recognize transitional apprehensions and provide whatever help is needed to nudge the process forward. You may need to be especially consistent, loving, and available to counter the negative forces that are pulling at the client. With persistence, and mutual effort, the **momentum** can be turned toward constructive change and away from past patterns.

Dependency

Another component of the intervention phase is increased dependency. Having earned the clients' trust during the beginning phase of treatment, it is typical to find that they will wish to draw from you more and more. The weaker their **identity**, the greater their dependency needs. This can be an asset more than a liability.

In the world at large, people foster dependency for mostly unhealthy reasons such as growth avoidance. As a consequence, when individuals become dependent, it usually comes to a bad end. In therapy, the emphasis is on healthy interaction, and when needed, healthy dependency. Dependency can be healthy, if it is temporary, growth oriented, and a means to a constructive end (Polansky, 1971).

Dependency is really nothing more than drawing from the ego of another person. If the clients' egos are particularly weak, then they have probably built a number of maladapted defenses to compensate. Growing beyond these defenses and finding new and healthier life patterns is what therapy is all about. Letting go of old identity, which is propped up by destructive defenses, usually requires that clients be able to draw from the support and identity of others. In this case, "the others" is you—the therapist. Most clients will need to temporarily pull from your identity as they build their own.

This dependency, unlike most, is **temporary**. You are working yourself out of this role even as you begin it. You are here to assist clients until they are more able to self start. During the intervention phase of therapy, it may actually be a necessity. Eventually, dependency is something that most seek to grow beyond.

Productivity

Achieving a good end to short-term therapy requires a great deal of productive effort on the part of clients and therapists. Change cannot be left to chance. Together, you must intentionally pursue productive directions. Productivity is at the core of the intervention phase of therapy.

By the time clients enter the intervention phase, most of the confusion has been settled. Goals have been established and their insight into their problems has filled out. From this foundation the client is able to strike out and take **active steps** toward change. They are able, but not necessarily always willing. They will have continued need for **direction** and **encouragement**. Still, at this time the clients' capacity for productive effort is substantial. If you have done your homework, they have the **strength and resources** to move forward.

During this period, the goal is to put thoughts and ideas into action. Clients have the ingredients and now is the time to mix them together and bake the cake. It is from this productive effort that clients are able to move toward the final stage of short-term therapy.

RESOLUTION PHASE

The final phase of short-term therapy is characterized by autonomy, creativity, and fading. The phase is exciting, in that it represents the completion of much of the therapeutic task. Equally important, the resolution phase determines the lasing value of the client's short-term therapy experience.

Autonomy

Paradoxically, the dependency that is likely to occur during the transition phase evolves to autonomy in later stages. Having drawn from the therapist for a time, clients become increasingly able to function **independently**.

During this time, clients will take more **initiative** and risk. They will find it easier to **assert** their position, although this may take the form of resistance or withdrawal (Gustafson, 1986). This testing of wings is generally just that, for clients are trying to test how well they can do without you.

Such autonomy should be supported and encouraged (Glasser, 1965). Clients are better off making independent bad decisions on occasion than not making any decisions at all (Rank, 1942). They may stumble, but the bumps and bruises teach lessons on gaining independence.

Creativity

Short-term therapy cannot produce all the answers to all client problems (Gustafson, 1986). Certainly, you can hope to address and resolve some of the more pressing ones. In itself this is no small accomplishment, but there is a carry over. The insight and skills that clients develop in addressing present issues have a broader application.

The ability to take general concepts, adapt and apply them to other situations is a creative process (May, 1971). As therapy progresses, it is common for clients to introduce new circumstances to which they have applied recently learned knowledge. It is like the adage—giving a man food, feeds him for a day; teaching him to grow his own, feeds him for a lifetime. The core principles of **IntraActive Therapy** can be **generalized** to a variety of life circumstances, and this concept is manifest in the latter stages of therapy.

One part of the therapist's role is to stimulate **creative application** of what clients have learned to their personal situation. You can do this by encouraging clients to seek out some of their own answers. Another way is to bring up old situations and test their application to current ones. Whatever the method, short-term therapy offers its best when there is a **residual effort** toward creative problem solving that remains long after therapy has ended.

Fading

People remain **bonded** to people who fill needs. If you and I do our job helping clients learn to meet their own needs, they will need us less and less. With successful therapy the need for continued relationship fades.

I use the word *fade* intentionally. I do not believe that a therapeutic relationship should terminate in the traditional sense. More realistically, that relationship should **evolve** naturally in new directions. As this process occurs, the intensity of the relationship, frequency of contact, and cruciality will decrease.

In the last stages of short-term therapy, clients will call less and begin to skip appointments. They will ask for your input less frequently and even show a little resistance to your offerings. Your approval will still be important, perhaps as much as ever, but they will be able to do without it. Knowing you are there will still be of continued value, though. Clients can venture far and wide just knowing there is a place they can come back to **renew** their batteries.

Fading is a constructive process. Like the dye on an old pair of jeans, the surface color may wash away but the jeans themselves are more comfortable than ever. Having been an important part in a client's life, you will always be—just in a different way. You have helped the client to face some difficult life problems and gain identity in the process. Anyone who does that stays in the heart for a long time.

CHAPTER 8

SOME PRACTICAL THERAPY CONCEPTS

INTRODUCTION

As you work to develop your own therapy style, you will also develop therapeutic concepts that make sense and work for you. You will find that the more practical these concepts are to your function, the more you will appreciate their value and support. What follows are twenty conceptual perspectives that frequently come up in therapy situations. They include information you can personalize, supplement, and use in your own good efforts as a therapist.

OUR DEFENSES BECOME OUR IDENTITY

Identity is a learned thing, and the body of identity is developed in our childhood. In the ideal environment, people are taught all of the skills and insights necessary to become fully functional adults. Some of the most important ones include:

1. The skill of communication. This includes the use of mouth, actions, eyes, and other senses.
2. The capacity to understand, respond to, and support the emotional self. Emotions need potty training too.
3. The ability to love and give of self. This is a food necessary to all people and ideally people should know how to give it to others and themselves.

4. The skill of constructive, intentional, and creative thinking. The mind may have lots of I.Q. potential, but it needs training to reach that potential.
5. The art of intimacy and relationship. Few things in life are more complex or necessary than how to deal successfully with other people.
6. The ability to do things. Knowing why, when, what, how to bring action to life is a skill that will be tested more frequently than any other.
7. The functional flexibility to adapt and grow. The best computers are those that can be reprogrammed to change as needs and demands change.
8. The capacity to enjoy and have fun. It is important to experience the depth of life and what it means to be a living human being.
9. The willingness to risk. People need to be open to success or failure to function fully in a complex environment.
10. The ability to learn. Those who seek new information, retain it, and use it are best able to face life on an ongoing functional basis.

If any of these life skills are neglected or mistaught, then people are more likely to experience conflict, failure, and rejection in the course of day to day living. No surprise here, as everyone faces these experiences. No child is taught all of the skills noted above. As a rule, however, the less people are taught the more they are vulnerable. The greater their vulnerability and resulting pain, the more likely they are to seek defense (Freud, 1961). These defenses can become more than a temporary measure for self-protection. They can become their identity.

No one likes pain, but everyone has it. If the measure of hurt experienced exceeds the capacity to handle it, then people begin to seek relief. They build behaviors that serve to screen them from the hurt they feel otherwise powerless to avoid. If the hurt is limited and temporary, then their defenses will take a similar path. If, on the other hand, the damage is long standing and deep, then their defenses become a more permanent part of their makeup.

In essence, in the absence of functional skills, people compensate with stopgap measures that give them temporary relief. Some of the more common defenses include:

1. Dishonesty
2. Anger

3. Denial
4. Fantasy
5. Isolation
6. Projection
7. Suppression/repression
8. Sublimation
9. Obsession
10. Fragmentation and psychosis
11. Distraction
12. Worry
13. Avoidance
14. Intensity

These defenses are much like a magic ring. If used long enough they take over the soul. The defense becomes a surface personality. Deep down there will be the real person, but for practical purposes, and in the eyes of others, the defended self is the one who will live out his or her life.

Successful therapy with most people requires that the clients' defenses can be identified and resolved in favor of more functional life skills. What should have been taught to the clients as children, when they were an open book, will now have to be taught to the adults, adults who are afraid and who have years of added pain and behavioral entrenchment. Now you see another reason why a therapist's task is so difficult!

EVERYONE WANTS ACCEPTANCE AND LOVE

Walk out into the world and find the meanest, cruelest character you can. You may see absolutely nothing in that person of redeeming value, but of one thing you can be assured—this person wants to be loved.

Everyone, no matter what age, sex, nationality, or background wants to be appreciated and cared for (Rogers, 1951). This seems to be a primal need that is as deep rooted as the need for food or desire to reproduce.

Yet, if you look at some people, perhaps even most people, this need for love is not apparent. In contrast, many people appear hardened to the idea and thoroughly distanced from anything so childish. Therein lies the key. What dies for most people is not their need for love, but their faith in love (Freud, 1974). To be more specific, some people lose faith in the loving nature of mankind or the ability to attract this love if it does in fact exist. In consequence, they become superficially blocked and emotionally shut down to their need for love (Freud, 1974).

This concept is crucial to the therapeutic effort. Even though the client before you may show no interest in acceptance, attention, and affection, (each of which is a cousin to love), remember that these needs exist. Penetrate the camouflage and surface defenses to the person within. The harder the individual, the more deprived the need. You cannot overcome the defenses unless you recognize that they exist.

Some people have been deprived so deeply for so long that they may seem unreachable. Sometimes the defenses are so hostile or destructive that the person is unapproachable. Again, remember that the need for love is still there under all that armor and it must be your decision as to how much effort you wish to invest in working through the layers of defense. Certainly, some people will not be reachable no matter what. Most, however, with patience and support that was not available at an earlier time in their lives, are able to gradually open the doors.

EVERY ESCAPE HAS A PRICE

In today's social climate we are surrounded with information about the dangers of alcoholism and other forms of drug addiction. Images of family turmoil, automobile accidents, destitution, or loss of health quickly come to mind as consequences of these addictions. Truly, many have followed the path of substance abuse and know the price to be paid on a very personal basis.

Substance abuse is only one of many escapes that are common to our culture (Sonnenburg et al., 1985). Many people become addicted to food, power, money, people, gambling, work, and other widely recognized escapes. It seems that human beings have the capacity to become addicted to about anything.

An addiction is something that attracts people through its capacity to distract and people are vulnerable to differing kinds of distractions. The depth of their addiction depends on what they are being distracted from and how deeply that needs goes. The greater the pain or void, the more it takes to dull the hurt or fill the emptiness. Knowing how tough life can be, it is easy to see how people can become victims of addiction. In probability, few get through life without periods of addiction.

Because this theme is a pervasive part of the human experience, it is important to note one of the primary principles of addiction—there are no free escapes. No matter what the tool, every distraction has a price that must be paid (Glasser, 1965). In some cases, this price is easy to spot. One need not gaze at a heroin addict for long to receive graphic evidence of the price paid for the relief gained. In other cases, the price is subtle or even invisible. Marijuana seems to be a good example. The loss of identity, motivation, and personhood that occurs with protracted use can be very subtle and difficult to measure.

Generally, the more distractive power the addiction offers, the greater the price that is paid for its use. In addition, the consequences are further magnified by the frequency with which individuals indulge their addiction. Power addictions that are pursued regularly can be infinitely destructive.

The destructive forces of addiction do not seem to be here as just a source of moral punishment. Rather, they serve as channel markers designed to force people back into the mainstream of reality. Were it not for the prices that escapes from reality command, there is no doubt that many, if not most, would pursue escape over real life. The explanation has to do with the difficulty that living in reality creates. Life is a difficult and demanding process that stretches skills at every turn. People are forced to either grow forward or retreat into escapes and are rarely allowed to remain in place. Like almost everything about life, escapes have a place. All human beings reach points where they need temporary relief or shelter. It is probably normal, natural, and necessary that they escape on occasion. Moderation must be a part of this process, however, and the consequences of escapes help encourage in this direction.

People who pursue therapy are people needing relief. It is likely that before they came to you that some addictive behaviors have occurred. Frequently your task will be to help clients identify their addictions, the price of these escapes, and ways they can grow beyond them. The real world is tough. The world of escape was made even tougher in order to force people back to where they belong.

SYMPTOM RELIEF IS NOT THE SAME AS PROBLEM RELIEF

In a typical hour of television viewing, at least two solicitations are received to buy an over-the-counter medication. People are encouraged to take one remedy for their headaches, something else for their digestive problems, and another drug for aching muscles or the heartbreak of psoriasis. These ads are slick and filled with assurance of relief. If one listens closely, he will hear that the relief promised has little to do with causality and mostly deals with symptoms. In other words, these medications might help in feeling better, but they do not do much to help you be better.

Advertisers who try to market over-the-counter (OTC) medications are not lacking in intelligence. They are responding to a cultural belief in magic and an overiding concern with the quick fix. What is going on behind the scenes does not matter as long as people feel better.

This concept has important implications for understanding and treating people (Allport, 1968). Most clients who come to you will be conditioned to seek symptom relief (Sifneos, 1972). Your task will be to help them in this direction, but to keep an equally strong emphasis on problem relief.

Previously discussed was the adage about giving a man a meal and feeding him for a day, and teaching him to grow food and feeding him for a lifetime. This concept typifies the importance of a focus on problem relief. If you help a man feel better, you get him through today, if you help a man become better, then you assist him through his tomorrows. Unfortunately, there is much about our culture that makes working toward problem relief difficult. On the average, people are more receptive to taking a pill for an emotional illness than to talking with a therapist about that illness. The same culture that emphasizes pretty tomatoes over tasty and nutritional tomatoes, or attractive cars over ones that work, or image over substance is constantly teaching people that feeling good is a primary goal. There is probably some truth here, except that the feeling good needs to be a by-product of living and doing good rather than an end unto itself. Much of the crime and substance abuse occurring in our culture is from frustrated people who are simply trying to feel good because they think everyone else does.

As you treat your clients, take care to not confuse symptom relief with problem relief. Both are important, but it is the latter that will carry your impact into the future.

PEOPLE RESIST CHANGE

In the earlier stages of life, human beings are highly vulnerable to the maladies and inconsistencies of their environment. Because few, as children, have sophisticated problem-solving skills, their systems respond instinctively to stress with a host of natural defenses. If their environment generates too much pain, their emotions move into a depressed state in order to reduce their agony (Gustafson, 1986). If rejected, neglected, or abused, people's systems develop anger to bolster their courage and help them feel integrated and in control. If their environment is overpowering and intimidating, they assume a dependent and passive stance that does not threaten the powers in charge.

These defenses may appear to be dysfunctional but can actually be lifesavers in the formative years. The rub comes later. Those very defenses that may have kept someone alive in the jungle become liabilities when that person returns to a more civilized existence. Just because the sources of stress are no longer present does not mean the defensive system shuts down. On the contrary, past pain is never forgotten and is anticipated for the future. In short, the defenses resist change because they fear for their owners safety.

It does no good to attack an individual's defenses. The greater the attack, the greater the entrenchment (Kadis et al., 1974). Further, you will find that most people are quite attached to their emotional defenses. They may not like some of the consequences of being defended, but those defenses have been a friend for a long time. Giving up their defenses is like turning their backs on an army buddy who got them through a war.

Resolving defenses is a process of retraining. As people try alternative coping methods that work, their inner self begins to trust their judgment. If, for example, they try being assertive over passive, and do not get crucified, then their defended self is more willing to give up the reins. As the scars can run deep, it is clear that retraining the inner self is a process rather than an event, and it can take years.

As defenses are addressed, it is important to recognize them as friends, not enemies. They may cause problems, but they exist for a reason. At some point they helped in survival. As we grow up, it is desirable to grow beyond defenses. Defenses may not want to let go until shown that a person is capable of more healthy survival tactics.

PEOPLE REACT TO LIFE IN PATTERNS

From the time human beings are born, biophysical, social, psychological, and environmental forces are forging their development. Each of these impacts on the other in such a way as to make predictability difficult and diversity of species assured. In general, the greater the stability or health of these areas, the less tumultuous the developmental process. Dysfunction in even one area can have far-reaching consequences. One such consequence can be patterning.

As children, people lack sophisticated cognitive abilities and experiences. Consequently, they are susceptible to programming that may be in contradiction to their basic needs. Forces that have an impact create images that become fixed and static. Cognitive and thus, behavioral reactions, can become patterned in a manner that lacks logic and flexibility. This process has been explained biochemically to the extent that in some people, parts of the brain that are alive and well are not used under some circumstances (Wedding et al., 1986). Certain circumstances trigger a habitual block that limits the thinking resources to a part of the brain that might be primitive, rigid, slow, etc.

A child that is abused, for example, is likely to develop a brain imprint that says everyone is a potential source of abuse. Thus, when this child advances in years, he will see a person, react with patterned thinking that tells him this person is dangerous, and be distant and cautious (Freud, 1974). His more sophisticated thinking resources are never tapped. It is something like calling the White House for the President's opinion on foreign policy and getting a tape recorded message regarding visiting hours. What people get may have nothing to do with what they need.

Part of the therapist's goal is to identify patterned thinking and open up the doors to the client's more advanced thinking resources. This is best done by raising awareness, reprogramming conscious thought efforts, and modifying behaviors. Overcoming these thinking barriers and limbering up unused parts of the mind can be a trying process, in that the brain will typically fight this risky expansion. The same person who was abused can benefit from hearing a trusted person say that everyone is not abusive. Such individuals can make an effort to try to think through reactions to others rather than acting on instinct. Then, the individual can try to behave differently, perhaps nondefensively, towards others in a way that will generate more positive reactions. With time, the patterned thinking is replaced with rational thought that better utilizes the full powers of reason.

MACHO, MATURE, OR MEEK—MALE IDENTIFY

Most men measure their worth in terms of their culture's current concept of what a man should be. Men follow these expectations in an effort to find acceptance. Considering society's inconsistencies in this area, it is most certainly a roller coaster to misery. Twenty years ago being labeled "a radical" was a manly thing to many people. Doing drugs was manly, and so was long hair and promiscuity. Now the majority prefers conservative thinking, no drugs, short hair and sexual restraint. It is not surprising that many men cannot figure out who they really are.

Most men who come for therapy are experiencing at least some measure of identity confusion. In today's climate, people are supposed to be a person first and then follow their gender path. That is fine, but gender is a force that must be acknowledged. Men are different from women. There are numerous contrasts, not the least of which is biological.

In helping men secure their identity, you can serve best by assisting them off of this roller coaster and by helping them make some decisions about who they are and want to be for the future. At the risk of over simplification, let us say that men basically have three options—to be macho, mature, or meek.

The macho man can be characterized as aggressive, in control, and self-directed. His ego is something to be protected at all costs, and he cherishes personal power. His models and images seldom come from the mainstream of society, and are sometimes lacking in sensitivity.

The meek man takes a more passive path. He sees folly in aggressive lifestyles and seeks to minimize conflict. The meek man is not necessarily weak. He may be unsure, unsupported, or just uninterested in a more masculine lifestyle.

Probably the third option, the mature man, is the most adaptable. In that the mature man avoids the extremes of macho or meek, he is able to respond to his world in a more natural and less fixed or reactive manner. This type of man can love, be sensitive, and commit, but he is also independent, open to risk, and able to face conflict effectively (Fine, 1988).

Whatever direction a man takes, it should be one he follows through intentional choice. Too often insecurity, a need to please others, bad role models, and old emotional scars dictate the attitudes men have (Widom, 1984). Filtering through these issues can enable a man to decide what is best for him and take his identity into his own hands.

IDENTITY

Having an identity is simply having some sense of who you are. It is having an idea of what you believe, what you can do, and how you fit into the scheme of life. Identity is knowing that you are separate and functional entities and that you count.

It is truly a tragedy of life that so many people go through it without having an identity, or if they do, one that is battered and fragmented. So if people do not have a complete identity, what are the options? Some people have a partial identity. In some places their sense of self is fixed and identifiable, while in others there are gaps and distortions. People who come from inconsistent backgrounds tend to have inconsistent identities.

If their backgrounds lacked in good models, opportunities, and support, then it is possible for them to have essentially no identity (Harris, 1967). This may be hard to believe, but everyone knows others whose behavior, values, or commitments change with the wind. These people have little or no true sense of self, reacting instead to their environment. They use their internal defenses and needs as an identity of sorts, but it really is not.

The saddest group of all are people who have what could be called a subidentity. These individuals have been damaged to a degree that their sense of self is entirely regressive and negative (Peck, 1983). Often they feel tremendous self-hatred and tend to be self-destructive as a result. A subidentity requires a background that is characterized by profound and chronic abuse. When people have a subidentity, they were targeted at an early age for malicious treatment.

Whenever individuals come to you for help, one of the first issues to explore is the scope of clients' identity. The greater the fragmentation, the more patience, support, and time you will need to invest. Like everyone else, these clients will be afraid of change. In fact, the less identity they have, the less willing they will be to risk. Some people's identities are just that fragile.

BURNING OUT ENGINES THROUGH INTENSITY

High stress environments encourage people to react with a heightened sense of awareness. Their bodies and minds perk up so that they might better respond to harmful or risky circumstances. When the stress abates, so too does their state of readiness. Simply put, they relax. When people are exposed to super intrusive stress (trauma) or protracted stress, they are forced into a super intense of long-term alert status (Rachman et al., 1988) For some, this condition can become a way of life. These people forget what it means to relax.

Combat veterans know about this reaction, and it is typical for abused children as well. Even though the outside may say relaxed, the eyes will tell us that something else is going on. The symptoms can include runaway brain, difficulty sleeping, fidgeting, low energy, constant movement and shifting, and general defensiveness. These symptoms can continue for years.

One way to defer this state of alert is to have clients imagine that they are a car. Their car has a five speed transmission. Those gears allow them to shift into whatever degree of pulling power they need to get the job done. An intense person usually stays in the lower three gears. At their most relaxed state, they are still putting a strain on the motor. Have clients visualize themselves shifting into higher gears whenever possible. The sensation is a little less pronounced, but very similar to what occurs in an automobile. When shifted into fifth, the car engine quietens, the strain decreases, speed increases, and there is a sense of greater efficiency.

First, second, and third gear people have been conditioned by bad yesterdays to anticipate bad tomorrows. They want to be ready so that they can handle what comes. With guidance, they can learn that shifting gears is not difficult, and that they have the resources to respond to upcoming hills and obstacles before they are harmed.

TIME FIGURES INTO GROWTH POTENTIAL

Time does not heal all wounds, but it does make it easier to take the steps to bring about that healing. The mature therapist recognizes time as a distinct ally. Neglected or abused children sometimes do not show graphic symptoms until they reach adolescence. Unfortunately, this is a period of tremendous emotional upheaval, physical transformation, identity formation, and marginal maturity and skills. Consequently, bringing about change during this time can be a very difficult undertaking. It is important to remember that everything necessary to therapeutic intervention is doubly necessary with adolescents. Double patience, double love, double commitment, and often, double time are requirements not to be forgotten. Even with your best effort, it may require the passing of time and your clients' youth for you to see the fruits of your labor.

Many character-disordered clients can also benefit from time. Character disorders are notoriously resistant to change. However, the greatest potential for change occurs when these individuals enter their late thirties and forties. Having experienced life, and their own inability to live it well, they are more open to change at a conscious level and more able to change at an unconscious one.

Time can work against people as well as for them. Time can conceal necessary truths and knowledge. Time can allow bad patterns to become entrenched and pathological. Time can place people under pressures that inhibit their ability to change and grow.

From any perspective, time is a crucial component of therapy. Make good use of the time you have with your client and recognize its strengths and limits. You may plant seeds for a long period of time before they begin to grow. You may never actually get to see the change you have helped bring about in another person. If you use time as an intentional resource, however, your success in helping will be all the more likely.

CHANGE AND FEELINGS

When people change their thoughts and actions, a change of feelings occurs. It is this change of feeling that both rewards their efforts and measures their success. Trouble comes when feelings do not move at a satisfactory pace. Then, people are left feeling frustrated and discouraged, sometimes assuming that the changes of behavior and thought are misguided or ineffective. Such a reading can be incorrect, due in part to the lack of understanding of feelings.

Feelings are notoriously unreliable. People have too little control over their feelings and too little knowledge of the true source to make feelings crucial to change efforts. People may be making great progress, but their feelings tell them something totally the opposite.

The feeling self can become programmed just like thoughts and actions (Ellis et al., 1977). Emotions get in a groove and find it comforting to stay there. Thus, when emotions change, they change reluctantly at best. They are afraid to adapt because experience has taught that the person they exist within is going to be hurt sooner or later, so why change only to change back again?

Then there is the issue of short-term and long-term feelings. Short-term feelings are like the wind. They come and go from all directions. Behavior and thought processes seem to have minimal direct influence over these feelings, at least to a point that can clearly be seen. Actually, even though it may not be apparent, thoughts and actions do have a major impact on feelings. It is just not as dramatic and tangible as people would like. If people direct their behavior and thinking toward a good or bad result, then emotions will change in kind. To secure change, they must have faith in this process and use their more tangible tools of behavior and thinking as measurements of their success.

As changes in short-term feelings occur and people begin to experience some emotional reward, they may hit a wall of sorts. This wall is composed of long-term feelings that are much more stubborn. If there have been years of pain and deprivation then long-term feelings are pervasively entrenched in a defensive posture. Depression, anxiety, and other protective emotions will be there telling individuals to keep their heads down. It can takes days and weeks to bring about changes in short-term feelings; months and years to change those which are long term. Fortunately, people can count on one law of personal change. When short-term feelings are changed, then long term feelings will follow suit. Those changes may be slow in coming, but persistency will bring results.

HIGH STRESS LIVING

As people go about daily routine, they have three directions they can take. No matter what the activity, they can coast, they can live, or they can push through the experience. The manner in which individuals pursue these options can have a dynamic impact on their level of stress and functioning (Rachman et al., 1988).

Coasting through an experience is like going for a ride with someone else as the driver. Things are allowed to happen and a limited amount of energy is invested in determining how they happen. When individuals coast, they conserve themselves and let life happen.

Living is more active. Living is being in the moment, experiencing it, and trying to nudge it in some direction. Living is not passive or dramatically aggressive. In living, things are made to happen, but also things are allowed to happen, and the experience is enjoyed either way (Yalom, 1980). Living is an end unto itself.

When individuals push they seek to force life in a desired direction. They channel their energies with the intent of directing the world around them. Pushers are movers and shakers. These people do not let it happen, they make it happen. This type of high energy lifestyle is demanding and powerful.

Coasting and pushing are extremes on either side of living. This is not to say that either one is bad, just that each represents opposing ends of the spectrum. As a rule, living is more stimulating than coasting, and less draining than pushing. Nonetheless, all three options are needed in order to be an adaptive person. Some situations require that individuals coast or push in order to be effective.

Stress occurs when too much time is spent coasting or pushing. Coasting, with resulting understimulation, and pushing, with resulting overstimulation, charge a toll. That is fine in moderation. The body, mind and spirit can afford and even benefit from the price. Too much time coasting or pushing, and the stress can cause damage.

Clients seeking to reduce their stress level can benefit from assessing how they handle their continuum of options. Likely as not, patterns will emerge that point to a need for change. Stress patterns are ingrained and not easily redirected. Defining their existence and targeting change efforts are a big part of this process.

THE RELATIONSHIP TRAP

Strange things are done to everyone in our culture, but nowhere is this more evident than in the education of women. For decades women have been put in charge of one of the most difficult facets of life—relationships. Women, by their nature or by their education, are thought to have greater strength and makeup for this responsibility. It is not fair or true, but it is a theme that seems to continue even in today's more advanced culture (Widom, 1984). Women, like men, are programmed toward roles that limit rather than empower.

In picking up the relationship gauntlet, it is easy to settle into patterns of interaction that are predictable and ultimately painful. Overburdened with an almost impossible task, some women adapt into harmful relationship patterns (Franks et al., 1983). Without great caution, it is easy to assume roles characterized by a tendency to endure, change, worship, control, or punish. Born of misguidance, confusion and frustration, these roles are seldom a source of fulfillment and happiness and lead to dysfunctional coping efforts (Wirken, 1988).

The enduring woman feels it her duty to accept and go along with the practices of her mate. She sees this as a responsibility of love that she must carry and so keeps her doubts and hurts to herself, quietly tolerating the absurdity. In doing so, she sells herself and the relationship short. As she endures, she surely wears out.

Some women approach their relationships with a sense that they should be accountable for problems their mate might have. They feel a responsibility to change their mate. These desires are generally not selfish, just misguided. It is not possible for a woman to change a man, or any other person for that matter, unless that person is even more committed to changing himself.

Other women are caught in a subservient relationship position. They put men on pedestals and make unreasonable sacrifices to the needs of these persons they have made their focal point. Those who are worshipped develop a distorted perception of their value and take others for granted. Thus, the woman who is subservient finds herself increasingly distanced from the one she seeks to love.

Knowing that a mate can cause harm, one way to stay safe is to stay in control. By various means of control a woman may feel safer from abuse or misuse. Safety may be achieved, but intimacy and appreciation will not. Men, like women, make poor pets and they seldom appreciate their owners. When nothing seems to work, some women get angry and punishing. They see anger as both a shield and a sword. If a woman has been hurt by other men who are no longer around, she can sometimes generalize her feelings toward someone who is.

As a therapist you will be faced regularly with relationship concerns. You can help by searching for these disruptive patterns and guiding your clients toward alternatives (Collier, 1982). Dysfunctional approaches are less a reflection of character than poor models, programming, and reactions to painful life experiences.

CONFLICT AND ADVERSITY

When human beings dream of their futures, it is usually with an eye on a stress-free existence. Their images do not include hardships and they exist in a situation that is peaceful and nurturing. Such musings are comforting during difficult times, but would people actually be better off living in a world without troubles?

Hardship is not an enemy. It is a teacher that stimulates people to develop and use their resources. Without it, much of the potential that people have would lie fallow. There was no gardening in the Garden of Eden, and you can better serve your clients when you help them understand conflict and adversity as natural, normal, and even potentially beneficial.

When people are faced with problems, they have essentially three response options. They can react from a passive, aggressive, or assertive position (Alberti et al., 1970). Through the first response, they seek to minimize their conflict by minimizing their resistance. They succumb to the pressures and allow them to guide their actions. Survival is possible, but rarely with a measure of self-esteem and identity.

Those who resist passivity, or are tired of it, generally seek an opposing reaction. People respond to conflict in an aggressive fashion and seek to eliminate problems by undermining the source. There are times when aggressive action is necessary, but this adversarial approach can generate as many conflicts as it solves. Of equal importance, aggressive living can become a way of life. The ability to live can be lost because of the addictive need to fight, overcome, and win. Aggressive people have a stronger sense of self than passive people, but they are not able to realize it through a happy life.

Assertive people are strong enough to fight, yet wise enough to do so in a selective manner. The goal of assertiveness is to cope with conflict and adversity, not win against it. When individuals seek to win, they make problems their master rather than a temporary distraction or intrusion. Assertive people can grow from hardship because they refuse to be hardened by it. When individuals are assertive they retain their dignity and identity, as well as the capacity of living life fully.

Once clients come to understand hardship as natural, they lose some of their sense of victimization. When they learn to face their problems in an assertive manner, they become more effective masters of their own fate.

ADDICTIONS

Much of the current thinking on chemical addictions focuses on the concept of disease. There is evidence that supports the existence of people who are physically more susceptible to substance abuse than others (Lader, 1975). This theory seeks to undermine the old concept of limited willpower and weak character.

The problem with the concept of alcoholism as a disease is that it supports the notion that addiction is something that happens to people instead of something that happens with people. I believe that the latter is almost always a factor in any type of addiction.

If individuals do have a part to play in their addiction, then what is it? Certainly willpower and strength of character are important, but rarely is it so simple. Further, limiting the focus to these variables allows for much blaming but not much helping. There are more substantial issues that can be targeted (Johnson, 1980).

The fact is that almost all addictive people have severe problems with anxiety and depression. They are addicted to whatever will provide relief from these feelings. It is for this reason that temporary success in weaning addictive people from their addiction rarely translates into long-term freedom of addiction. Removing the chemical is just the first step. Treating the underlying causes of anxiety and depression is where long-term success is found.

People with addictions are practicing self-medication for a problem they often cannot define, understand, or handle. In treating any addiction, your task as a therapist will be to help clients curtail the addictive behavior, as well as root out the underlying causality. For years, therapists tried unsuccessfully to treat addictions with psychotherapy while failing to note the importance of managing addictive behavior. When therapists gave that up, they made a dynamic switch to behavioral management and seemingly forgot the issue of underlying pathology. The last thrust has been toward biochemical methodology and the disease model.

Actually, none of these approaches can stand alone. When you are facing addicted clients, remember that you are also facing people who are anxious and/or depressed. They will get relief constructively, with your help, or destructively, through their addiction. People get physically addicted to chemicals, but beneath it all their greatest addiction will be to their need for emotional relief.

LIVING OUT ROLES

From their youth, people are encouraged to assume roles compatible with their environment. In families, they may find themselves playing the role of mediator, trouble maker, or victim of circumstance. These and other primary roles serve a purpose and are usually assigned by others or self-assumed as a defense. Within limits, some roles can be constructive, giving the power to impact on an individual's environment. Out of check, roles can stifle identity and channel actions in directions that betray spirit and potential.

Roles are like computer programs; they guide behavior and encourage people to function in a certain fashion. Roles can be comforting in that many decisions are predetermined and risks are minimized. Without the balance of caution, it is easy for roles to replace personhood.

Many homemakers have diligently pursued their roles as mother, wife, and protector, and in later years found themselves taken for granted and unappreciated for their efforts. The resulting emptiness and loss of identity are reasons why so many women in this country use some form of psychoactive drug.

Mishandled roles can be equally harmful to males. Too many men marry and father children because they feel they are supposed to versus genuinely wanting to. With time, they grow resentful of the trapped feelings they experience and typically ventilate their frustrations toward their families. Substance abuse, affairs, and other distractions help them endure their roles, but that is not the same thing as living real lives.

It is best to be an individual first and then assume desired roles. Jane is an individual who happens to be a teller. John is an individual who happens to be a nurse. Children are little people whose roles supplement their life, not replace it.

Probably one of the primary causes of the high incidence of depression has to do with the lack of positive identity and its resulting dissatisfaction. If roles have been dictating who individuals are instead of the reverse, then some form of unhappiness is a guarantee. Pay particular attention to the roles your clients play and help them get off the stage and into life.

LIVING THROUGH OTHERS

Most forms of dependency are a reaction to childhood deprivation (White, 1986). A lifetime can be spent trying to meet old needs. The emptiness creates pain, and relief can be the primary motivation for living. As children, people live in a room with open windows and doors. Other people like parents, siblings, schoolmates, and teachers can enter this room freely. The love and acceptance received from their visits leaves a lasting impression. Throughout people's lives, they will remember how good it felt to be supported by others. Even if there was a minimum of endorsement, the impression of even rare moments of love never leaves.

As children grow, those doors and windows slowly begin to shut, until at some point in adolescence they are completely closed. Even though people are not aware of this transition, it is permanent. From this time until they die, the only person in their room is themselves. They are the only ones with the power to determine their self-worth and identity. Others can reach them through their doors and windows, but they cannot come all the way in. The influence of others will be limited and not as powerful as it once was.

It is rare when individuals realize the transition they have undergone in growing up. Most people continue to seek the endorsement that once meant so much. Lifetimes are spent seeking relationships that will heal past damage and fulfill unmet needs. All the while they are unaware that the only hands that can do justice to these needs are their own. They are the only ones left in the room.

This process is the foundation of most forms of dependency. Not knowing the reason or the futility of the effort, people continually look to others for relief. It worked once, when they were younger, why can't it work now? People can live a lifetime and never realize that the natural dependency of youth cannot be successfully duplicated in adulthood.

Your role as a therapist is to assist clients in recognizing their position of responsibility. Others can help and close relationships will always be important. It remains, however, that effective responsibility for identity, value, happiness, sense of being loved, purpose in life, or any other major aspect of personhood cannot be assumed by any other person. Clients are the sole masters of their destiny.

When, as therapists, you facilitate this sense of reality, you can then help your client build the skills needed to carry their fate (Glasser, 1965). It takes both skills and a personal responsibility for a client to become his or her own person. Facilitate these two forces, and you break the dependency cycle that is the cause of so much harm to so many people.

DYSFUNCTIONAL EXPOSURE

This world has its share of toxic wastes. There are the obvious poisons that are found in chemical dumps, polluted rivers, and hazy air. However, more dangerous poisons come from toxic people.

Toxic people are not necessarily bad people, but they do bad things. They have been harmed by life and corrupted by their psychological defenses and need for relief. These are not people to be shunned, though. Were it not for the damage they cause, they should be pitied (Peck, 1983). There, but for the grace of a higher force or chance, many could have gone instead.

Rarely will you have an opportunity to treat a toxic person. These people avoid treatment and seldom pursue it responsibly. It is too hard. They are too deeply entrenched to take the risk. There are exceptions, and you should give everyone a chance, but those exceptions are very few in number. Even though you may not be able to reach toxic people, you can reach those they have affected. Your intervention can help stop the cycle of toxicity and restore normalcy to their lives.

Clients who have been touched by toxic people will require great patience. Their sense of reality will be distorted. They will have poor role models to draw from, and their coping methods will be marginal or dysfunctional. These damaged people will see pain as a way of life, and will probably not even know that their experience is unique or abnormal (White, 1986).

Your task will be determined by the amount of poison they have received and the level of continued exposure. People will break away from dysfunctional environments when they understand what is wrong and how to change it. Dysfunction has the magnetic power of the familiar, but hope and success carry a greater force.

Dysfunctional people have an investment in perpetuating their species. The more the world is like them, the less they have to fear. These people resist personal change, but they also like to keep others at their level. To do anything else is to risk exposure and a loss of power. Dysfunctional people, families, or cultures do not give up easily.

Emotional illness, social dysfunction, and behavioral maladaption are simply symptoms of poisoning. At times, the poisoning has been chronic, with heavy doses that do deep personality damage. Finding and administering an antidote will be difficult. At other times, the exposure is more subtle and superficial. In either case, defeating the impact of dysfunctional environments will be the focus of your therapeutic effort.

LEVELS OF RELATIONSHIP

Relationships are a strong determining factor in early development and eventual quality of life. These interactions with others can be defined in terms of quality, quantity, purpose, and impact. Still another framework has to do with level of intensity. Relationships can be divided into superficial, personal, and intimate categories. All three serve a good purpose, and each is a necessary ingredient for successful social interaction and personal development.

Superficial relationships are characterized by limited depth and purpose. They involve no risk interaction around issues that require minimal social interplay. Relationships with grocery clerks, service station attendants, or people spoken to walking down the hall are probably superficial relationships. These relationships are necessary to accomplish some tasks, but also to help test the waters. Most social relationships begin at a superficial level in order to get a sense of the other person before determining whether a deeper level of relationship is desired.

If more closeness is pursued, the next level would be called a personal relationship. These relationships entail greater risks due to sharing ideas, perspective, thoughts, and attitudes. People probably have personal relationships with doctors, next door neighbors, and co-workers. They are personal relationships because deeper thoughts are shared, and riskier in that others may not share common opinions. Much of what gets accomplished in this world is accomplished through personal relationships.

If people are able to develop a successful personal foundation with someone, they may consider moving to the next level which is an intimate relationship. Intimate relationships are characterized by a sharing of feelings. It is at this level that the greatest potential fulfillment is achieved. By sharing feelings, doors are opened to the deepest areas of vulnerability. At best, relationships with parents, spouses, and best friends have achieved this intimate level of interaction.

Normal development requires a measure of each level of a relationship. Whatever people were exposed to as children is what they typically feel comfortable with as adults. If everything was kept superficial, that trend is continued. If there was a personal relationship with their family, individuals are better able to risk personal relationships with others. If there was a good measure of early intimate interaction, people are usually more comfortable and effective at this third level.

Some never leave the superficial level, while others remain stuck at a personal one. Ideally, everyone should be able to achieve some solid exposure to the third level. It is at this level that people begin to thrive, understand themselves, and experience the joy of loving and being loved.

Most therapeutic relationships have elements of each of these levels, thereby serving as both a model and a source of practice. Your task is to help the clients transfer their relationship skills and willingness to risk from the therapeutic over to their real world.

FROM THIS DAY FORWARD

Changing today and tomorrow is not possible without letting go of the past. For many, the walk through life is characterized by the accumulation of failures, hurts, mistakes, and transgressions. Whether created by others or themselves, people carry the burden of past inadequacies in a pack upon their backs. With time, they become so weighted down that they have little energy to go on. Life becomes an endurance contest to be survived and tolerated until it ends.

People who are going to change must look at their past with a forgiving eye. There will certainly be failures, but having occurred in the past, they must remain there. To continue self-punishment for those errors is to guarantee continued failure (Rogers, 1951). The pain created through old guilt prohibits energy and hope necessary for successful change.

When individuals seek to change they must start with a foundation of self-support. Since so much of what is not okay about people was created by others, or done through a lack of awareness, they have to be tolerant of who they have become. Certainly individuals must admit their mistakes, but that is very different from continually punishing themselves. People may not like who they are, but they have to take themselves for what they are. They must accept and support themselves and then begin to grow toward their new goals. It is not possible to hate themselves now, and be any better off tomorrow. People cannot reject themselves into being better (White, 1986).

Personal growth has to start from this day forward. No one has walked in others' shoes, and thus, no one has the ability to judge with fair accuracy. Much like nurturing a lost and sickly puppy back to life, there must be self-nurturing in order to heal wounds. An old dog **can** be taught new tricks. In the case of people, those who have lived in pain and difficulty for long periods are often more able to change than those who have not. These people know that what they are doing does not work, and if they can be shown a new way toward hope, they will embrace it.

Human beings cannot live without stumbling. If they curse themselves for those falls, they are even more likely to be distracted and repeat their errors. Each day is a new day, and must be treated as such if tomorrow is going to be better than yesterday.

CHAPTER 9

MAKING A GOOD THING BETTER PRACTICAL THERAPY ISSUES

INTRODUCTION

As a therapist, your role is a complex one. You are faced with an array of variables that preclude an easy task. What follows is a summary of many of the practical factors that influence your development, success, and fulfillment as a therapist.

WHO CONTROLS TREATMENT

You have spent years trying to become a positive source of direction and help to people. Therefore, it makes little sense to forego your training and knowledge and place the therapeutic process in the hands of your clients. They come to you for the support and insight that they cannot find elsewhere. In doing so, they are offering you a license to enter their lives and effect change. Use that license with courage and confidence. You limit your capacity to help if you fear this responsibility.

Client-centered therapy does not have to mean client-directed therapy. Most clients need you to be a supportive partner who takes the lead. The control that they or others have exerted has not been successful or therapy would not be an issue.

Not all clients will appreciate your efforts to lead the process. Some may resist the risks involved in giving another person a measure of control. They do not know what to do, but they will be afraid to let you do anything either. This resistance is normal and simply one of many hurdles you must address.

Directing the therapeutic process is not the same thing as directing someone's life. Your task is to influence the process, not dominate the person. At times, this may feel like one and the same. Not so—one is a task that you are trained for; the other is a responsibility best left to a higher power.

LISTENING VERSUS TALKING

One of the safest therapy techniques is listening. Listening can communicate concern, provide support, and encourage intimacy. Listening is a primary skill that all therapists should develop. Listen not only with your ears, but also with your heart and eyes as you try to hear what your clients are really about. Listening can have a profound impact on individuals, but this should come as no surprise. So few people have the opportunity to feel heard or understood that they delight in those rare moments when someone listens. Listening can raise clients' senses of self-worth, help them ventilate bottled up emotion, and bond them to relationship with you. It is clear that listening serves you well in your efforts to help.

Without discounting the contributions of listening, it is legitimate to recognize that listening is not enough. Most people need more support and direction than listening alone can provide. Talking, sharing, and advising are also necessary.

Providing therapy to other people can be a risky undertaking. The potential for failure and frustration is high. Helping clients grow is not like repairing a broken car part. People are more diverse and idiosyncratic. As a consequence, many therapists prefer a nondirect approach to therapy which minimizes their vulnerability. Unfortunately, the therapist's own need for safety may limit therapeutic change.

People come for answers. You do not have them all, but you do have some. When tempered with concern, maturity, and responsibility, your advice can effect great change. Most clients will appreciate your willingness to talk to them about what you think they should do. They know you can be wrong, but in coming to you for help they have already made some decisions about your credibility.

Talk to your clients as much as you listen. The percentages will vary from session to session, but clients need to hear your input as well as share their own feelings, needs, and perspectives. Responsible advice from a concerned and informed resource is hard to obtain. Few people are in a better position to offer this kind of input than you, a trained and experienced therapist who tries to be genuinely committed to the needs of your clients.

CONFIDENTIALITY

As you spend many hours pursuing clients' openness and honesty, it is not unusual to become desensitized to the power of what you learn. What clients tell you, including everything from routine biographical data to innermost secrets, is sacred to some degree. The clients' need for privacy may be inflated or misguided, but, with rare exception, their need for confidentiality should be respected.

If clients are dangerous to themselves or others and in abuse situations, you have the right and responsibility (legal and otherwise) to violate confidentiality. No therapy issue is totally black and white and confidentiality is no exception. There may be other times when you believe that a spouse, parent, employer, or other significant person needs to know something that you have learned privately. Whenever possible, you are well advised to clear things with clients before sharing information with others. You may think what you wish to share is innocent or insignificant, but when you make this judgment casually, things can become unpleasant in a hurry.

Confidentiality is one of the key foundations of therapy. Most people who come to you place privacy as one of their top five priority needs. Violate that privacy and you destroy their trust and your relationship.

It is a good idea to get written permission to share confidential information. This is awkward, but in today's legal climate it is necessary and prudent. A signed letter of permission to release necessary information is one legal safeguard. As a rule, blanket releases do not protect you as well as releases obtained each time you share confidential information.

Make it a habit to avoid sharing clients' information with your spouse, friends, and others. Even disguised information can be deciphered and targeted toward your clients. If, as a therapist, you talk a lot about others, the word will get around and people will question your reliability as a person who respects confidentiality. It is all right and sometimes helpful to use the experiences of some clients to help others, but be careful to protect confidentiality as you do so. Remember that just being able to keep clients' secrets makes you unique and valuable in their lives. Take care not to violate that position.

AVAILABILITY

Typical contact with a therapist occurs on a once-a-week basis. During a period of crisis and change, a week can be an eternity. Being available in the interim makes the difference between a hurdle overcome and a hurdle that overwhelms.

As a therapist, you may be further along in your own process of growth and development than your clients. You may not remember the feelings of aloneness and apprehension that commonly go with change. It is helpful if clients know that there is a point ahead when they will have contact. This lends a measure of security to their efforts to risk change. Having better access can further accelerate this willingness to risk.

Being a therapist is a way of life more than a job. As such, involvement with your clients is not limited to a nine-to-five schedule. Problems occur after those hours, and I personally see value in being partially available during these hours, as well. My appointment card has my home phone as well as office number. My clients are told how they can have me paged, and that pager is with me essentially twenty-four hours a day.

At first glance, this kind of availability would seem to be somewhat unfair to me as a therapist. After all, it would seem that providing access twenty-four hours a day would not leave me much room for private time. Surprisingly, this is not the case. I find that my clients are almost always considerate of my time and privacy, and rarely contact me unless there is a strong reason to do so. Yes, I do get an occasional 2:00 AM call, but usually it is for a good purpose. That call can catch things early, before the client's situation has deteriorated drastically.

It is for you to decide if you feel comfortable being available after normal working hours. You will find that your efforts to be available will usually be rewarded with appreciation and increasing client autonomy. You will be able to intercept problems before they mushroom and actually sleep a little better knowing that major issues are not brewing in your absence.

Being available does not mean that you are open to misuse and abuse. Occasionally you may have to set limitations for some clients who misunderstand your availability and take advantage. Nonetheless, the occasional intrusions that result from being accessible are far outweighed by the advantages. Your willingness to be available will set you apart from many of your professional peers, and demonstrate a level of concern that is a unique and powerful change agent.

CREDENTIALS

This may not have always been true, but recent decades have produced a greater measure of competitiveness among various therapy providers. Each professional group claims to have skills or knowledge that another does not and thus assumes a position of professional superiority or exclusiveness. It is unfortunate that therapists who purport to be experts at people problems would pursue such a regressive path.

Credentials are a statement of professional accomplishment, but they cannot begin to affirm you as a competent and effective therapist. Examinations may test your knowledge base, but knowledge and its application are only one small part of being a good therapist. The review process that you go through in obtaining licensure and certification sets you against various criteria and screens you out if you do not match up with these specifications. These screens were not designed by clients, but by educators, trainers, administrators, therapists, and others whose agendas are very different from clients seeking help. How many questions do credentialing exams have about compassion, availability, and honesty? Contrary to the rhetoric, the goal of the typical regulatory body is less to insure the needs of clients than to purify a respective profession. The reasons are simple. Exclusivity protects the profession and insures longevity. That is a concrete and specific goal that a regulator can clearly identify. What it takes to make a good therapist is a more controversial and diverse issue that is less easily addressed.

To simplify, credentials are nice and they say something about certain milestones you have reached. They are not, however, the total measure of professional development and to make them so is a misguided effort. An overemphasis on credentials fuels professional competitiveness and establishes artificial hierarchies. Psychological tests that have poor validity are rarely afforded credibility. The validity of credentialing is certainly up for question, yet therapists are almost frantic in their efforts to prove their value with these pieces of paper. I am not convinced that degrees, licenses, or other such credentials make any therapist better than the rest.

BOUNDARIES

One of the greatest forces impacting on the active and involved therapist has to do with boundaries. Boundaries are the limitations that must be placed on the various levels of interaction that occur with our clients. Setting these limits is difficult. What is appropriate for one client, such as a hug, may be totally inappropriate for another. Although the ethical guidelines set by most professional organizations are distinct, little else about life is, and professional boundaries are no exception.

There are several boundaries that can be put in place that are almost always appropriate.

1. Do not misuse your client. Certainly therapy is a mutually beneficial relationship, but make sure you have a primary focus on your clients' needs.
2. Avoid having sex with your clients. Much has been said about the damage that sexual relations can render to clients. Realistically, this damage seems identical to that which occurs in any major relationship that is handled immaturely. Harm is harm, however, and as a therapist, you are here to help. **Steer clear of physical involvements with your clients.**
3. Clients are rarely more emotionally intimate than with their therapist. This intimacy can lead to natural feelings of increased respect, emotional attraction, and love. After all, people tend to love those they know best and this is one of the fundamental goals of therapy. As a consequence, it is not uncommon for therapists to develop the desire for greater emotional intimacy with clients. Pursue these feelings cautiously. These emotions are not wrong, but do need to be channeled. An intimate personal relationship is different from an intimate professional one. Stay with the latter and you protect your clients and yourself.
4. Keep things as honest as you can. Dishonesty, with good intentions or not, rarely contributes to good therapy outcome. Do not say things you do not mean or believe. Your clients are going to have trouble trusting you if you are a bit too flexible with the truth.
5. Do what you can to help your clients, but when you cannot find solutions, seek out recourses that can. This one is tough in that few of us like admitting our limitations. Nonetheless, it is extremely unfair to your clients to keep them in therapy beyond the point where you can give them what they need. Failure to refer can be a professional ethics violation, but more, it is a failure of good faith and concern for your clients. Your job is to help your clients work through problems or to find the help they need when you cannot.

Learning your professional boundaries is a difficult part of your development as a therapist. You will have to explore your own abilities to find those that seem appropriate. In view of the potential for harm, approach your boundaries with caution.

PERSONALIZATION

IntraActive Therapy is an attempt to define and simplify the short-term therapy. It represents a strong effort to quantify and make practical what can be a very confusing and trying process. Any time a model of therapy is developed, there is a tendency to try to make everything fit that model. This effort to label and process people can be counterproductive. Therapy should be conformed to individual needs, not the reverse.

IntraActive Therapy is concrete and pragmatic, but one of the greatest strengths of this model is its capacity for personalization. Any therapeutic process you undertake should be designed around the individual you are working with and your own skills and knowledge.

Another element of personalization has to do with treating the client like a person while being one yourself. It feels good to be a learned scholar whose advice is sought far and wide, but remember that first and foremost you are a human being. Your powers of influence will increase if you hold to your humanness.

Clients generally respond better when they feel they are receiving care that is genuine and adjusted to their needs. Being a name on the schedule does not bring out the same response in clients as feeling they are important people whose needs and personhood are a sincere priority.

DOCUMENTATION

Documentation is one of the more unpleasant tasks facing most therapists, but it is a necessary undertaking for a number of reasons:

1. You live in a litigious society. Leaving a "paper trail" of your professional efforts can help to protect you in the event of such a problem.
2. Sometimes it is difficult to remember important client information, especially if you see a significant number of people. Your ability to retain details will improve over time, but written records can help support your memory.

3. If your services are covered in part by health care providers, they may request documentation about the course of treatment, diagnostic information, etc.
4. Documenting your impressions, plans, and actions can help you frame a treatment process. To document, you have to quantify, and this can strengthen your focus and implementation efforts.

Describing treatment on paper is not the same as providing treatment. It is not uncommon to find organizations or therapists who develop elaborate documentation but are found lacking in follow-through. Documentation is not an end unto itself, but rather an augmentation of your most intentional effort—effecting change and resolution. Therefore, organize your documentation in a way that is practical and manageable. Stay on top of it in a manner that supports versus distracts from your therapeutic efforts.

FEES

There are several factors to consider when you are establishing a fee procedure. Several of the more important are:

1. Consider the normal and customary charges for your particular discipline in your area. You need not be bound by this reference point, but it will generally reflect a rate that is in keeping with economic and professional conditions in your community.
2. Make a living. All professionals should donate a significant measure of their time and energies to those who cannot afford full fees. Keep this work in balance, however, as major responsibility combined with minor income can be a critical burnout equation.
3. Whatever fee you set, be clear with your clients. Hazy fees and payment procedures create confusion, mistrust, and irresponsibility. Informed clients are more responsible clients.
4. Charge everyone at least something. Invariably, free service is taken to mean marginal or mediocre service. Charge people within their means if that is your belief, but you will find that people who invest their money and time will appreciate therapy more than those who invest only time.
5. Stay on top of clients' charges. As fees pile up, it places a strain on the

clients and the therapist. There are ways to encourage clients' responsibility for their accounts without communicating greed or a lack of concern.

6. Keep the financial side of your practice in balance. Fees are just one of the rewards of being a therapist. Money alone is a poor motivator and it will not carry you forward in your practice. Keep income in perspective with giving, growing, and productivity, all of which contribute to your professional fulfillment.

REFERRALS

For most practitioners, the three primary sources of referral are previous clients, other professionals (physicians, school counselors, attorneys, etc.), and the phone book. Each of these referral sources has advantages and disadvantages.

Referrals from previous clients are one of the best measurements of a successful practice. If a former client refers a friend, then he is saying that you helped him in a positive way. One of the problems encountered with this type of referral, though, is that new clients may come in with unrealistic expectations. Their friend was "fixed" and you should be able to do the same for them. A plus with this type of referral is that it requires no investment of time or money, and the third party (referrent) is minimally involved.

Referrals from physicians and other professionals are the foundation of many practices. Physicians are in a position to discover people in need yet they have limited time for in-depth counseling themselves. Three or four therapy-conscious physicians can provide a sufficient referral base for an average practice. The primary disadvantage of this referral source is the accountability to a third party. After physicians have used you as a resource, they will understandably look for results and feedback. Their expectations and philosophy may come into conflict with your own over issues like medication usage, or cost and time factors. With good communication, these limitations can be managed, and it is generally worth the effort.

The yellow pages can be one of your cleanest sources of referral. Although your advertisement will need to be tailored to the client population you are seeking, a good ad can stimulate a strong referral base. Yellow page referrals have no third person to satisfy and the self-referral itself implies motivation and desire. Many times, however, this enthusiasm is short-lived and only a temporary response to crisis. Yellow page referrals should be acted on as quickly as possible. This effort is not to pull people into therapy who do not need it, rather to recognize that their window of pain can be temporary even when their problems are not.

Regardless of the source, treat all referrals the same. There is a natural tendency to respond more actively to easier, powerful, monied, or connected clients; however, giving all of your clients equal enthusiasm and energy will best support a lasting referral base.

CONTINUING EDUCATION AND TRAINING

It is amazing how quickly the trends in therapy change. Information that was state of the art five years ago can be old hat today. New and exciting knowledge and methodologies are being presented in rapid succession.

On this basis there is no question that graduate education is just the beginning of your professional development. Continuing education is more than a pesky requirement for credential renewal. It is about keeping you alive and productive in your efforts to be a constructive therapist.

There is a popular trend among licensure boards to take the position that if a therapist has not been trained in a specific area, he should not practice in it. On surface consideration, this makes sense. It does take skill to be a therapist and to make effective use of the diverse treatment tools available. It does not, however, take fifteen years of guruship to master each of these tools. You have been through graduate school, and although you may not know everything, you do know how to learn, how to generalize, and how to apply what you have learned. These are sophisticated skills that can help you make good use of brief continuing education exposures.

The availability of continuing education is one of the better success stories of the helping professions. Most areas of the country have private and public sponsored learning opportunities on a regular basis. Use them! A stagnant pond does not support active life as well as one that is continually replenished with fresh water. The same is true of therapists when they become stagnant or isolated. Continuing education stimulates the mind, guides actions and enhances success in what a therapist does. Anything that accomplishes all that is a necessity, whether your credentialing board requires it or not.

COMPETITION AND PROFESSIONAL CONFLICT

Psychotherapy is a product of this century and practically speaking, the last half of this century. During this period this form of care has gone from rare to routine. The number of therapists, theory options, and disciplines of practice has exploded. Such evolution cannot occur without some revolution, and sadly, much of this energy has been directed into professional against professional. Therapists, like many helping professionals, can sometimes match Wall Street in terms of competitive and hostile spirit.

Being people and living in a world that can be harmful, tends to make all individuals innately insecure. As compensation, they naturally seek power and control over themselves, or more frequently, the world around them. The greater the sense of control, the less the feeling of insecurity. Nowhere is this better manifested than the manner in which professionals seek to contain, manage, and sometimes stifle their peers. You will not have to be a therapist for long before you realize there is a hierarchy, based largely on academic degree, that sets therapists up in a pecking order. Even chickens are instinctive enough to determine their pecking order through power and contribution to the species.

Therapists stake out their turf on the basis of something as limited and notoriously inconsistent as graduate education. In doing so, good is defined as the capacity to endure academic programming (I spent five years on my Ph.D.!) versus productive effort (I helped five people feel better today!).

Actually, therapists are no different from any other group that exists on this planet. People tend to compete and worry too much about the other guy. Therapists are supposed to know how to help others live better, yet they are repeatedly guilty of the same mistake. If anything, therapists make that mistake more effectively because of their people skills!

Try your best to stay away from running down your peers. If you think they are wrong, have the courage to say so, but choose your method and timing wisely. It is just as important to keep your motives clean. Try to work harder on doing what you do than on undermining the efforts of others. This is a big world and there is room for many styles and viewpoints.

An eye toward productivity and less competitiveness can make your life easier. It helps you control yourself, which is a task that you can accomplish, and it helps you avoid trying to control others, a frustrating task that you cannot accomplish. It is interesting to note that in the absence of professional hierarchy and competitiveness, it is found that there is infinitely more commonality than contrast.

ENERGY AND CONSISTENCY

Anyone who has been a therapist for long realizes that it is not an easy or low energy task. From the perspective of the uninformed it may seem that all therapists do is listen to people, but the reality is altogether different.

The burnout rate among therapists is tremendous. The day-to-day grind of facing client problems, major responsibilities, and fighting the routine hassles of professional practice can easily become overwhelming. Becoming a therapist is hard. Staying one is probably even harder.

There are a number of ways that you can keep your energy and consistency alive. For starters, remain a friend to yourself. Being a therapist takes courage. You will be faced with many dilemmas and stressful situations where you need yourself as backup and support. Question what you do, but with an eye toward support and encouragement, not criticism and constant doubting. Studies have shown that many therapists experience what is termed the "imposter syndrome." Under these circumstances therapists discount what they do and feel like charlatans. No doubt some are, but most are not. If you try to be a concerned and helpful therapist, then you probably will be. You may not move mountains and enlighten mankind, but you will probably have a good impact. Being your own worst critic will blind you and feed your burnout.

It also helps to keep your support system alive. Investing time and energy in your family, friends, and colleagues will keep your perspective and mental health in balance. Isolation and loneliness can substantially undermine your continuity.

Be careful about going through the motions. Trite as it sounds, you will receive no more than what you put in. Making your profession a hobby or means to other ends will rob you of the stimulation that purpose and meaning provide. Long-standing therapists are typically individuals who make it a point to be dynamic and invested in their work.

Take care with your priorities. Being a therapist for money, power, or the like will not sustain you for the long-term. The motivation provided will not be sufficient to the demands of long-term practice. There is nothing wrong with making money or having constructive power. Both are visible signs of a successful practice. Just make sure that love for others, unselfish giving, commitment to creative endeavor, and growth are included. It will be much easier to remain in the arena when many of your fellow therapists have gone elsewhere.

HUMOR

Humor is the capacity to maintain perspective in a lighter and more positive vein. This is not to be confused with immaturity or lack of responsibility. Responsibilities can be treated seriously while you retain a counterbalancing sense of humor.

We live in a world of the serious. People worry, obsess, and agitate over everything. It is as if doing so somehow makes them more important and lends some sense of control to that which they cannot control. This seriousness creates pressures that distort perspective and undermine energies. Humor is an elixir that puts everything back in place.

As a therapist, you will encounter many serious issues. All of them will require responsible action on your part. Very few, however, will warrant an overzealous response. Get too serious and you may tend to get myopic, rigid, and ineffective. Do not blow things out of perspective and become part of the problem. Most obstructionists, for example, are well-intentioned and serious people trying to do what they think is the responsible thing. Instead, they just get in the way.

By looking at the lighter side of things, you can keep your perspective and flexibility. It is easier to save your energies for the things that really count. A sense of humor is a skill that can be developed. No matter how serious or sour your approach has been, you can begin switching things immediately.

Clients respond to humor. The thoughtful application of this tool can defuse tension, establish intimacy and trust, and provide comfort and pleasure to clients that may have little of either. Most clients are already too serious. Pain makes people that way. They need a beacon to lead them out of their darkness. Adding one cold, dark, wet blanket to another creates little additional warmth. A sense of humor, on the other hand, can bring some badly needed sunshine.

FAMILY MEMBERS

Family members can be an asset or a liability to therapy. If they are healthy and secure people, they will usually support a responsible therapeutic effort when they have an understanding of the methodology and goals. Unhealthy family members, in contrast, may be threatened or intimidated by your client's efforts to change.

In crisis, most families will flock to support a client in trouble. They will want that person to get well, but sometimes not too well, especially if the client's wellness forces change on the family. When this happens, your role as change agent is likely to be challenged or undermined by dysfunctional family members. Remember that survival is paramount to the neurotic individual. Start undermining the family's neurotic patterns, even if it is for the good of the client, and you will go from being the "nice doctor" to the "quack" that is making her crazy.

Sometimes family conflict is unavoidable if you are to truly help a client. You can limit or avoid this conflict by actively including the family members when feasible. By making them a supporting part of the therapeutic process you are in a better position to keep them informed, nonthreatened, and motivated toward helping your client. It is a temptation to limit your focus to your client, but remember that he does not exist in a vacuum. Family members helped create some of the problems and they are powerful influences that you cannot afford to ignore. In fact, the sicker the family, the more important it becomes to try to make the family a part of your treatment efforts.

The therapeutic relationship is a marriage of sorts, and just like the real thing, you have to accept the in-laws. If you alienate or avoid family members, you may lose your client no matter how competently you address his needs.

EXPERIENCE

Yes, it is true that experience enhances professional competency. Doing something repeatedly conditions and teaches like no classroom can ever do. If you are a practiced therapist, appreciate the experience that you have gained. It is of great value.

But what if you are a beginning therapist? Your experience is largely limited to knowledge passed on by others and some minimal hands on exposure. Does this mean that you are not yet competent to practice? Certainly not! Experience is an important variable, but it is not the only one, and there are ways you can compensate for lack of experience.

Enthusiasm is one of the great resources of the inexperienced. A master logger may cut down a tree with twenty cuts of the ax, while a novice logger may take forty. Experience makes for efficiency, but the tree falls in both cases. The fresh and excited energy of enthusiasm can make things happen while the contained energy of experience remains in place. In the therapeutic context, clients find hope and support when a therapist is motivated and enthusiastic about helping.

Another compensator is the flexibility and willingness to risk that comes with limited experience. There is room to gain new insights and undertake efforts that a more experienced person might overlook or ignore in favor of the familiar. Most revolutions and dynamic inventions come from those who are fresh and inexperienced.

In summary, do not underestimate yourself because you lack experience. You will have that with time, and meanwhile, you have many other resources to help you be a good therapist. Others may discount your abilities, but you need not. Credentials on the wall may look impressive, but they collect dust and say nothing about what that person accomplishes when sitting opposite a client. If you are a new therapist this does not mean you are a bad one. Recognize the difference and use your resources with a measure of pride.

WORKING WITH CHILDREN

As a therapist, you will likely face numerous opportunities to assist children. You will be asked to conduct assessments and determine the need for play therapy, supportive individual therapy, and/or other therapies suitable for children. There will be times when this course of action will be appropriate. Take care, however, that in treating children you fail to address the true source of dysfunction.

Children are not born in a void. What is true for most adults is even more true for children. They are products of their environments. If a child is having problems, almost always the source can be traced not to the child, but to the forces impacting on the child. When you are asked to intervene just with the child you may be directed away from the real problem.

As a matter of practice, I tell clients or referral sources that I do not do child therapy. I do parent-child therapy. I must have the freedom to work with the child and the parents. In actuality, the process usually becomes parent-child-school-sibling-neighborhood-extended-family therapy.

When you are working individually with children, next to helping turn their environment around, the most important thing you can do is love them. Make coming to see you a warm, fun, and special experience. Play therapy is a good assessment tool and it provides an opportunity for a child to act out emotions and experiences. More than anything it contributes warm and accessible adult attention. Most children do not get their quota of love from adults. Your direct interventions with the child will have a positive impact if you give this and a little more.

WORKING WITH DIFFICULT CLIENTS

Some clients, by nature of their defenses, personality, or condition will not be easy to work with. To succeed with these people you will have to stretch your energies, attitudes, and patience. Following, are some of the more difficult patient populations and keys to working with them.

Substance Abusers

1. Press for the truth. Denial (which is simply truth avoidance) will be one of your greatest hurdles.
2. Work with their support system. You will find the people who enable their alcoholism and allies to help you help the client.
3. Do not take their attacks, lapses, dishonesty, mood swings or other symptoms too seriously. Alcoholics tend to make others feel responsible.

Paranoid Personalities

1. Take baby steps in everything you do. Keep the intensity to a minimum as this feeds their fear.
2. Be ultraconsistent in your support and affection. Clients are paranoid because they have been hurt and fear more hurt.
3. Spend time rebuilding the trust bond at the beginning of **every** contact. If you are not a trusted friend first, you will be nothing later.

Adolescents

1. Keep your interactions as interesting, purposeful, and fun as possible. Boredom will be your greatest enemy.
2. Maintain contact by phone in between sessions. Your attention will make you a unique adult and communicate genuine concern.

3. Do not forget the family and external environment. Therein lies much of the source of the teenager's troubles.

Character Disorders

1. Try to avoid their games. They will try to build you into their dysfunctional patterns.
2. Remember that lack of or distorted identity is the culprit behind most personality disorders. Help them redirect their efforts and build a better identity.
3. Much of the dysfunction that comes from a character disorder is an ingrained psychological defense designed to protect. Be a minimal potential source of hurt and you can help alter those defenses.

Co-dependent People

1. Avoid rescuing by helping them help themselves. No matter what they want you are not their rescuer, but a guide to help them accomplish this task.
2. Be patient and loving as it takes time to change. Co-dependent people are that way because of emotional voids and scars from the distant past.
3. Be as direct and confrontive as you are supportive. They need strong direction from a concerned source. One without the other will not work.

Schizophrenics

1. Do not believe that they will not respond to therapy. High energy, task-oriented, and positive therapy does work with this group of clients.
2. Work with their support system. Most schizophrenics are facing their illness **and** environmental dysfunction.
3. If they are on a medication, make sure they take it. The side effects are a concern, but the symptom relief can lay the groundwork for your work on problem relief.

Many therapists have certain client populations they prefer to work with. They specialize in work with alcoholics, children, or some other group. Although you might be more comfortable with one type of disorder over another, consider the importance of balance in your therapy practice.

Working with one group can enhance your ability to work with another, and burnout seems to be less of a factor with a heterogeneous client involvement. Even though there are some significant differences among disorders, at the core there is much more commonalty than you might recognize.

LEGAL CONSIDERATIONS

Therapists function in a highly legalized environment. The growth of the profession, abundance of litigation-minded attorneys, improved awareness of client rights by the general population, and the expanded role of regulatory bodies have helped create a legal mind-set that can encourage responsibility, apprehension, and/or terror among therapists.

Realizing that legal consequences may follow inappropriate action nurtures accountability. When therapists feel unreasonably vulnerable to legal attack, their sense of responsibility can develop into one of uncomfortable fear. States with overzealous regulatory boards can respond to the manipulations of disgruntled or frustrated clients who may, inaccurately, see the therapist as the source of their woes. When this fear becomes chronic, therapists can reach a point of apprehension that commands and stifles their actions. They become afraid that their therapeutic efforts will bring legal admonishment. Therefore, they do little or nothing that will incur risk. **A therapist cannot do therapy without risk.**

Certainly most people who become therapists are willing to take the risks. There are several ways you can maintain your commitment to productive effort and protect yourself in the process. First, pursue controversial or unique therapies carefully. Consult with colleagues and chart your course thoroughly. Do not avoid new ways, but proceed cautiously. Second, be especially careful with fractious, hostile, or manipulative clients. These traits are not always discernible, but when encountered, make sure you respond in deliberate and thoughtful fashion.

Make sure you keep up with the basics. Maintain an honest practice and document your efforts by leaving a paper trail of what you do. Be aware of the ethics constraints that your discipline adheres to. Some will seem absurd and so limiting as to preclude successful therapeutic effort, so if you elect to bend those rules, and almost all therapists seem to, take care that you have good reasons.

Finally, do have good liability insurance. Be honest when you apply; otherwise, it is likely you will lose coverage when your application is routinely reviewed in a litigation situation. For example, many policies do not cover cases of client sexual abuse, an area of particular vulnerability to the therapist.

Even though litigation is an increasing reality for therapists, the number of successful cases is relatively small. You are much more likely to be threatened or harassed by a client or state board than actually called to accountability in a court of law. To be fully insulated and protected, you would also have to be ineffective. Be responsible about what you do, but do not let the fear of legal entanglements stop you from doing it. In any case, remember that your first priority is your profession.

JUDGMENT ERRORS AND MISTAKES

We live in a culture that is sometimes perfectionistic in tone and judgmental in attitude. Any therapist functioning in this type of environment is subject to tension and apprehension. Why? Because in attempting anything as difficult as therapeutic intervention it is impossible never to make a mistake. I have certainly made them and so has every other therapist I know on a personal basis. You have too, or at least you will if you become a serious therapist.

In any human endeavor, mistakes are normal. To be mistakeproof you would have to be immobile and anything but an agent of change. To effect change you will have to take risks and venture beyond the familiar. Do either and there is a possibility for error. As a therapist, the rule of thumb is to make intentional and informed decisions that maximize growth and minimize harm. If you follow that rule you will still make errors, but they will not carry the weight of your successes.

There is a paralyzing trend among some to attempt purification of the helping professions by establishing fixed standards of behavior. These guidelines are held forth as safe, ethical, and, therefore, good. In this case, good may be to the exclusion of effective. Closed systems contribute little to the outside world and tend to choke themselves to death. The real world is not always fixed and perfect and neither are therapists.

YOUR COUNSELING SETTING

The physical setting from which you operate prepares the stage for more substantial issues. Although you will not always have control over your counseling setting, you may have some influence. Most organizations will allow for at least partial personalization.

Clients will initially judge you by the setting where they first see you. Their judgments may be inaccurate, but those first impressions count. The more your counseling setting offers a positive reflection of your abilities, the better. We all have different tastes so there are no absolutes that will insure client acceptance of your setting. There are, however, several themes that will help you in this direction.

Comfortable chairs are a must. You need one, and your clients need one as well. Make sure the chairs have back support and give consideration to placement. Have clients face you from a distance that keeps discussion on a more intimate level.

Your setting should not only reflect you as a therapist, but should also help to target your desired client population. People feel comfortable in environments that are familiar. An upper middle class professional will not appreciate your lava light and frayed curtains. A fellow who drives a truck will care less about your bank lobby decor, but he will appreciate the fact you have a coffee pot. Consider your client group when you try to design your physical setting.

Colors are important. Creams, grays, and subdued pastels are relaxing. Darker colors are a bit depressing, and some of the greens and whites can make your office look and feel like a barracks.

Put your credentials on the wall where they can be seen. Clients take comfort in these confirmations of your background. Have them framed and mounted in a neat and professional fashion. Let the rest of the room look as you wish, but use your credentials as a visible professional touch.

Plants, aquaria, rugs, and art work all add warmth to your setting. It says that you, too, are a warm person, and your clients are looking for that assurance. Make it a point to give your setting intentional thought. You will be spending much of your time there and so will your clients. The message you wish to send should not be left to chance.

THE REACTIVE PRACTITIONER

From the moment you become a therapist, you will be on the receiving end of clients' expectations. They will have images and needs they will assign to you. Most will do so subtly and adapt if you do not quite meet their standards. Some, with extreme needs or insecurity, will feel disappointed and even betrayed. In either case, you will feel pressure to be what your clients want you to be. Do not do it!

Your task is to explore the ways to be a good therapist, develop a model you trust, and pursue that model in an ethical and enthusiastic manner. In doing so, you will be developing your effectiveness and professional identity. This mission, if you should elect to accept it, will repay you with purpose, adventure, and fulfillment. If, on the other hand, you turn it down to become a people pleaser, you will likely experience some degree of professional burnout.

As a reactive therapist, you give up control of yourself. Your effort is to hear the needs of your clients and to try to make them happy. In taking this path you fail to recognize that what makes people happy is not always what is good for them. You will further discover that what people want changes from day to day and person to person. If you are not cautious, you will become like a tennis ball—bounced from court to court. Your primary task is to help your clients, not please them. If you can do both, all the better, but always put being of good help first on your agenda. Your clients may not always understand or like your efforts, but the results will more certainly garner their respect and appreciation.

SPECIALIZATION

Just as there are many approaches to therapy, there are many types of clients and needs. You may find that you have a special talent or interest that you are especially good at or particularly enjoy. You may elect to specialize in a certain type of therapy or to work with a certain client group. Examples of specialists would be family counselors, child psychologists, forensic psychiatrists, and clinical social workers who function as sex therapists.

Generally, specialization is more possible in populated areas. Specialization requires that you have a good client base to draw from. You might also find it easier to specialize in a public or government institution that specifically needs your skills.

Some therapists elect not to specialize, preferring the stimulation and variety of a general practice. As a rule, these therapists feel that working with one group actually enhances effectiveness with another and that therapy skills are transferable.

Specialization can simplify the therapists' tasks but sometimes to their detriment. Working with the same client population for years can encourage burnout. On the other hand, if you are committed to your specialty, do it well, and enjoy it, then burnout should not be a factor. If you do chose to specialize, make sure to back up your interest with appropriate training and continuing education. Both will facilitate your competency and keep your fresh.

TAKING IT HOME

Many student therapists have dropped by the wayside because they felt they were overly sensitive or prone to getting wrapped up in people's problems. The theory is that sensitivity and concern make individuals poor candidates for becoming therapists! If sensitivity is the capacity to feel, then therapists cannot be too sensitive. Certainly, sensitivity must be balanced with maturity, judgment, and a sense of priority, but those skills are more easily developed than sensitivity.

The fact is, you **should** take your daily client experiences home. If you have done your job, you have been close to your clients and have moved and been moved by what you have shared and learned. You do not want to turn that human experience on and off like a light. If anything, you might treat these feelings as you would a radio. Nudge the volume down, but stay tuned to the same station.

Remember, too, that you do not just sit all day and listen to people's problems. You help them develop and implement solutions, then get on with their lives. This is exciting involvement not a burden that you must drop before you leave the office.

You will find that the more you must distance yourself from your practice the more you will come to resent it. Your practice will become a source of intrusion to escape instead of a source of purpose and fulfillment. If you need a lot of distance, then there is something missing in your work.

Of course, you will need a break now and then, but your goal is to explore some new experience, not escape from your profession. Your work is one of the most important and healthy parts of your day. You want that good influence to carry over. So go ahead, take your feelings home with you. You will be bringing something more satisfying than a cold pizza.

WORKING WITH GROUPS

Group therapy skills are a valuable resource for the short-term therapist. Working with clients in groups saves time, money, and resources. Group involvement provides exposure to peers that individual therapy cannot. Groups are also excellent environments for your clients to practice what they have built through individual therapy. Leading a group requires certain skills that can tax your knowledge base. There is less margin for error in the group setting, and more people depend on your abilities to guide and facilitate.

Energy would head the list of group leadership skills. Making things happen with a group requires that you project your efforts toward diverse individuals. You must capture the attention of a number of clients, assess their respective needs, and channel their interaction in a productive direction. Groups are not a sit back, take it easy, and let things happen situation. Since everyone cannot be the center of focus at any given moment, a successful group leader must be able to facilitate member participation. A sense of humor, an accepting approach, and a purposeful manner are some of the tools that help keep people intrigued with a group even when they are not the focal point.

All of the elements of individual therapy are equally important to group therapy and sometimes more so. Because there is more than one person, the intensity is diffused and so too is the impact. A good group leader is able to make sure each member's involvement is meaningful enough to hold his attention. Group therapy is not "watered down" individual therapy.

Sometimes homogeneity is helpful because the group's efforts can be more easily defined and channeled. On the down side, there is a danger of becoming myopic and self-limiting in this type of group due to lack of diverse input. Heterogeneous groups will be less compatible, but remember that well-handled conflict is helpful, and everyone has unique insights and perspectives.

Although group therapy can be threatening, do not overlook this treatment resource. There are many groups out there, but you might also notice that they come and go. Groups are easy to begin, but less easily sustained. As a consequence, many therapists stick with an individual therapy model they find comfortable. In that groups are an excellent approximation of the real world, clients may be deprived of a primary resource for change. Make sure you have given groups a fair trial before you drop this productive treatment resource.

STAYING POWER

Like most life endeavors, the uninformed image of being a therapist differs markedly from the reality. Because helping people change is hard work and rarely a low energy effort, many therapists are lost in whole or in part by the wear and tear of demands and responsibilities.

You hope to be able to remain a therapist for the long term. You will be needed too much to let all of your training and experience go to waste due to burnout. Here are some vitamins of advice you can take to insure your staying power:

Try to keep it all in proper perspective. Treat situations responsibly, but not so seriously. The world is a place of absurdity that eats people up if they react with too much intensity. Keep your focus on what you can and should control and let the rest alone.

It helps to keep your heart in a good place. Do not hold on to anger and resentment. Instead, reserve your passion for efforts that are constructive and loving. Remember that you are one of the good guys, and do not lose sight of your desire to be a positive force in this world.

Make sure that you continue to grow and keep your channels open to change. A closed system stagnates and becomes threatened by the outside world. Remain a vigorous therapist by pursuing new ways and means to help your clients.

Believe in yourself. Try to be good at what you do, but do not measure your value through the eyes of others. You will make mistakes and people notice those more than successes. They may judge you unfairly; therefore you must take their criticism with caution. History reveals that there is rarely a pleasant reception for that which is new and different regardless of its merit.

Go about your efforts with patience. You cannot be the therapist of the year overnight. Many of your goals will come quickly. Others will take time.

Have some fun with yourself and your practice. As a therapist, you have a rare opportunity to touch and be touched by people. Enjoy this process and learn to soak up the pleasure of people.

You are working hard to be a therapist. Those are skills that should not be wasted. Set your sights for the long term. You need to be around for a long time, making it a better world by helping the people in it.

CHAPTER 10

FROM THE CLIENT'S PERSPECTIVE

INTRODUCTION

It is fascinating to hear clients' open perspectives on therapy. Such information offers special insight into the accomplishments and changes that can occur in a therapeutic relationship. Following are clients' responses to questions, as written in their own words. In each case the writer was encouraged to be honest about how he or she felt about therapy. The questions asked were:

1. Why did you come for therapy and who sent you?
2. What was your first visit like?
3. How did therapy compare with what you thought it would be?
4. How did you feel about your therapist and his method?
5. What did you like about your short-term therapy experience?
6. What would you change or improve upon?
7. What were your immediate gains?
8. What has the long-term impact been?
9. How would you summarize your therapy experience?

BETTY—AGE 86

My doctor arranged for me to see a counselor. I was becoming more and more frightened of people and withdrawing. I felt that I needed some counseling before my unhappiness got worse.

The young man I saw was nice. I remember how softly he spoke. He came to see me in my room and we talked for about an hour. He had my chart and asked me a number of questions. I tried to describe how I was feeling and he seemed to understand. When we were finished talking he told me that he thought I was depressed and unhappy. He also said that I seemed to be losing my confidence. Talking with him made me feel a little bit better that day. He seemed to understand and wanted to help.

The counselor was younger than I had expected. I had never been in counseling before, but it was pretty much like I thought it would be. I thought he was a nice man. He seemed to like his work and he was always enthusiastic when he came to see me. He seemed to concentrate whenever we were together. I did not feel like he treated me like a senile old lady.

I do not really know what short-term therapy is. I saw my counselor four or five times. Talking with him helped me to not be so afraid. He would always ask me to do things after he left and I tried to do them. He asked me to do things like going to activities and inviting other residents to my room. His pushing helped me to do some of the things I had stopped doing. I do not know what I would change. It would have been nice if he had not always been in a hurry.

I started feeling better sooner than I thought I would. My life got back to normal. I am still not sure what happened to me, but I did get really down. I am not sure how, but I know that staying in my room made it worse.

I hope I can keep feeling good. We have an arrangement where I can call him if things get bad. I did that a month or so ago and he came to see me again. It helped to talk things through, and I felt better when he told me that I had not slipped back to where I was before. It helped me. I wish we had more time to talk, but it was helpful to have someone to talk to who seemed to understand. I have his card and can call if I need him. That helps too. I think I am going to be OK.

ADRIAN—AGE 35

My family practice physician first sent me to my therapist because I was unable to get on top of things and to move ahead in life due to my low self-concept. My physician and I both agreed that some short-term therapy might help me begin to pull my life together.

When my physician told me of the therapist he wanted me to see he referred to him as a social worker. When I heard the term social worker I envisioned the health department and poor people and therefore felt uncomfortable as I anticipated my first visit.

During my first visit with my therapist he asked me questions about my family and friends, my schooling, my activities, as well as my physical and mental health. From what little I was able to tell him, I was surprised at how much he gleaned and how accurate he was in his picture of things. I remember thinking "Here is someone who really understands me." At the end of our first hour together I remember asking my therapist if I could have another appointment at the end of the week.

The foundation of trust is the key ingredient that holds our relationship together. Whenever I get hurt, I have a sense he will not turn his back on me.

I like my therapist's easy going and laid back style. We usually begin our hour on a light note with several laughs and a good joke or two, and then progress to our more serious talk time. Another thing I like about my therapist is that he tailors the therapy to suit my needs. I do not get the sense that I am being fitted into the same box as everyone else. I think the only thing that I would change about my experience in therapy is something that has already been done for me by area burglars. That is taking the phone out of his office, so that my therapist can devote his undivided attention to my case, during "my" hour.

My first accomplishment as a result of entering therapy was completing my last year of school (from which I had previously dropped out) and obtaining a job upon graduation. Long-term changes which have occurred as a result of therapy are that I am more in control; also I am learning to be more of a friend to myself—that learning never ends. Therapy generally has been a very positive and rewarding experience, as well as a lot of hard work. I have come away with a much stronger sense of who I am and who I can be.

SANDY—AGE 21

My mother talked me into seeing a therapist when she realized that I had been suffering from severe depression and when my problems started to interfere with my job, my relationships with other people and my self-control. I had suddenly became violent and self-destructive. I had lost all self-control. I would fly off into a fit of rage anytime. I felt as though I was losing control. I have always resented being controlled.

My first visit was difficult for me due to my unwillingness to cooperate. I had been self-destructive as a teenager forced into therapy at 15 and again at 17. Therapy had failed then and I could not believe that it could help some years later. My first visit with my new therapist was hampered by my feelings of fear, confusion, anxiety, anger, and guilt. Fear from failing past experiences, confusion mainly due to the reasons I was there, anxiety from anticipation of what it was going to be like, and if I could make it work this time, anger for having to return to therapy after several years, and guilt stemming from the reasons I had to return. I was emotionally and physically stressed out on my first visit. I had waited for too long to seek help and realized it immediately when we began to talk. There were no comparisons between my first visit with my new therapist, and what I had built up in my mind. A small office, very relaxed atmosphere, and small talk that eventually led up to what I wanted to say. I was not pressured into giving any information about myself that made me feel uncomfortable. There were not any tests or tape recorders, and there was not any outside interference or pages of paperwork to fill out. I was reassured again and again on my first visit that I was not being judged and that I had nothing to be ashamed of (the key message for someone like myself). I was informed that therapy would be frustrating and painful and would take time, commitment and hard work. I was informed that in order for therapy to work for me, I had to work with it. I was also informed that therapy could be long term or short term depending on my willingness to cooperate. I was also reassured in my first visit that the content of our sessions were strictly private and confidential and would not be discussed with anyone else. The only obligation I had was to myself. I could drop therapy at any time if I felt that was what I wanted to do. My first visit left me feeling secure and hopeful.

Anyone who is able to keep me in therapy is nothing short of incredible. My therapist's method is definitely one of the main reasons therapy is working for me. His constant reassurance and honesty has brought me through some hard times. Being controlled and having to deal with a unstable lifestyle has contributed to my downfall with depression. His allowing me to share some of the blame with others who are partly responsible has definitely relieved some of the anger towards myself. He has this way of helping you help yourself without you realizing you have done it. He is always telling me "I am your buddy, not your mother, not your father; just yours. You can trust me." He talks to me, not at me—on a level I can understand.

I did not feel as though I could begin therapy on a short-term basis. Short term to me meant a time limit. It somehow seemed impractical to someone like me who had been in therapy on and off for years without results. It had taken me a long time to come to terms with my problems and therefore I knew it would take a while to work through them. I was afraid of being pushed. When I discussed how I felt with my therapist he in turn explained to me that he wasn't going to set a deadline for me. We could take all the time we needed; but he had discovered that many times once a person came to terms with his problems he did not need as much time as anticipated. He explained to me that therapy did not have to be long and drawn out to be beneficial, but it is not an overnight success. It all depends on how well you communicate with yourself as well as each other.

I wish I had not waited as long as I did to seek therapy. That is probably the one big thing I would change and I would definitely be more committed, as I have not always been so. I have been weary at times. During crucial moments I have been withdrawn often when I found myself revealing things about myself I had never discussed with anyone or when I find myself changing. I always come around and it gets easier all the time. My therapist is very patient.

My immediate gain was a sense of relief. Knowing I was not going to have to deal with my problems alone anymore. Knowing he was there for me; I was not there for him. I have always had control over our discussions. Most important being understood, having someone there who can relate to what you're saying and going through, having someone say you're special, you're not alone and I am here for you.

To summarize my experiences during therapy is difficult, but this is saying a lot. Every visit is different and sometimes the experiences are satisfying and relieving. More often than not I leave my therapist feeling a lot more together than I did when I arrived. There have also been times when therapy has been painful and frustrating, but all my experiences, both good and bad, have been rewarding. I can say this looking back on the past year and recognizing the changes that have taken place.

RANDY—AGE 44

I came to therapy because I felt I had no other options. I came because of marital difficulties. It was the hardest step I have ever made. It turned out to be the smartest. In this culture, for a man to admit he needs help is very difficult. My wife may have pushed me over the edge in asking for help. She went to see a marriage counselor alone. I just remember feeling relieved after I had set up an appointment. I was lucky. I took control of the selection process of the therapist. I could have ended up under the influence of someone who could have confused me more. My wife went to a religious therapist who advised her to read the Bible and pray. I had tried reading the Bible and praying. We ended up with a therapist who turned out to be intent on people taking control of their lives as soon as they are able.

I finally found someone who cared and would listen. He not only listened, he really seemed to hear me. For a long portion of the beginning, I talked. Along the way he shared I was not the only one. It was not just me, as I had been told.

I felt relieved at the beginning because I felt I really had someone who cared and would help. I learned that I was not giving myself and others a break. I was too judgmental. Some of the perceptions of myself were unrealistic. I still fight those perceptions, but now I know how and continue to learn different methods to keep them from stunting my growth. I came to therapy as an atheist and with a mind-set on past failures. My major crossroad was when I stood up to my Dad. I just told him how he hurt me when I was a child. Even though I did this as lovingly as I could, this act threw my entire family upside down. I had broken control and said this life is mine. I then set up rules in which my family and other people would have to follow in dealing with me. Then I started the process of forgiving them and my anger started ebbing away. My anger started out directed at them; however, I had carried it around so long that it turned inward. I was angry at myself. All of this was under the influence and support of my therapist. I am now working on my relationship with God by working on my relationships with other people and me. My mind-set is shifting more and more from the past to the present and future. I try to use the past for guideposts instead of an anchor.

My goal is to "walk my talk" using Christ as my model. I am also learning to use other people as models. This way I can use their pasts as guideposts. There is no reinventing the wheel. This has not been a straight line uphill climb. My progress looks more like the chart of the Dow Jones stock averages. I feel like God set it up this way. Without the valleys how would I know the peaks. How would I get stronger and grow in faith? You will go crazy if you do not try. From what I have seen, I can not think of a better Hell.

The more I help other people, the fewer problems I seem to have. It doesn't matter who I help or how. As long as I help them on their journey and help them maintain their self-worth. This does not mean agreeing with everyone or being a doormat for someone. I feel I also have a responsibility to practice love. One way can be for me to love me for myself. Even when I make a mistake. No one has the right to punish me for my mistakes. This is a hard one for me. There appears to be a cycle here. If I see I am trying to think of ways to punish others, I am doing the same to myself. When I see I am punishing myself, I can also see I am thinking in this mode toward others. I use this to keep myself out of this loop. I am working on turning my dependencies over to God. That seems to be a life-long process. However, I feel this is important. We all have these dependencies. If we transfer too many of these dependencies over to others, it makes their behavior too important to us. I have enough trouble controlling my behavior without accepting responsibility for others' behavior.

I am forty-four years old now, and in many ways my life is just beginning to be my own. I do not know exactly; it does not matter. I used to feel guilty for not going earlier. Then I looked around and saw the number of people who are still in their self-made hell and I felt lucky. Actually, my life was not totally self-made. I probably had the help and influence of significant others. I do not think I could have done it by myself. I know it would have taken much longer. But then, it is not over yet. I still hit holes and have to climb out with the help of God and others.

One of the most important skills I am developing as a result of therapy is reframing. There can be several perspectives of one's action or behavior. Now I try to look for them, thus giving myself and other people a break.

In a one-year period I was fired from a good job, lost another one because a company went bankrupt, and my wife divorced me. I feel lucky. According to psychologists, I should have had two or three heart attacks.

Sometimes I feel like the little boy who came to his Dad and said; "Dad, I am afraid I flunked my math test today." His Dad said, "Son, that is negative. Think positive!" "Dad, I am positive I flunked my math test!" So, short-term therapy did not save my marriage—it saved my soul. I have come a long way. Maybe further than anyone in my family for several generations. I do not know. It does not matter, this is not a race against one another. Yes, I came from a dysfunctional family. I guess we all have to deal with that plus the cultural stuff going on. To make life good we have to deal with it in ways that we grow intellectually, physically, emotionally and spiritually. When we do this, people around us grow also. My life is getting better and better.

TRISTAN—AGE 15

After living all my life with my mother, I had recently moved to live with my Dad, step-mother, sister, and brother. My parents sent me to my therapist because of my troubles at home. I had made a suicide attempt prior to moving to my father's. I needed help to cope with my problems and adjust to a new life up here.

I hated my first visit with my therapist because I had never been to a psychologist before and I was scared. I remember thinking to myself that I was not going to talk. I felt that what was going on in my life was none of his business. However, after my parents left the session and I was alone with the doctor, I did open up some and started to talk to him.

It was a lot of different from what I thought it would be. I thought he was going to be some mean guy, asking a lot of questions and pressuring me to answer. It was nothing like that. He was very nice and he asked me just talk to him about my problem in Alabama. I learned that I could trust him when he told me that he would keep what I said in confidence particularly from my parents.

Since I have never been to another therapist, I really do not know enough to compare methods. However, I do not like the way he sometimes repeats himself in our sessions. I also do not like the way he spends too much time with my parents because it takes away my time with him. I like knowing that once a week I can go in and talk with someone who listens, helps, and cares. The support is nice. I feel that I could have benefitted from the therapy exactly the way it's been done and I do not know how it can be improved.

My school grades came up from failing to a B-average: my feelings about myself improved as I discovered ways to like myself; in conjunction with this, I started to lose weight and actively participated in my weight loss program; I improved my social life by learning how to get along with others; also, living with my dad became easier because I was beginning to open up to him and the rest of the family.

I realize that I had a major attitude problem that not only affected me, but also the people around me. I now realize that feeling bad about myself, feeling that people would reject me and my defensive ways were sources of my bad attitude. I have worked on learning to like myself and not to be as defensive when I am in troublesome situations. I have learned that by liking myself others will like me too. Another benefit of my therapy is learning how to communicate with my family, friends, and acquaintances. I have learned that being open and telling the truth helps me establish better relationships with people.

I feel that I have had a good experience because I am a lot happier and can get along with others. I have learned to talk about my problems more openly. Sometimes things get a bit boring, but being in therapy has helped.

CHAPTER 11

A QUICK REFERENCE GUIDE TO PSYCHOTHERAPEUTIC MEDICATIONS

INTRODUCTION

Psychotherapeutic medications serve an important role in the treatment of emotional illness. They are the treatment of choice for a number of disorders and the utilization of psychotherapeutics will gain speed in the face of their ready availability, minimal costs, and widespread acceptance.

If you treat individual psychological problems, you need to have a working understanding of these medications. If you do not prescribe, you need not be concerned with the molecular make up of a medication, but you do need to know the side effects, dosage ranges, and purposes.

In this chapter is provided a guide to most of the current psychotherapeutics in use. It will serve as a practical information source if you are not familiar with psychotherapeutic medications and as a quick reference guide if you are. Stay within your training and expertise with these medications, but remember that when you are treating clients, you should know something about any medications they may be receiving. Even if you are not the one doing the prescribing, you will want to be an informed participant.

ANTIDEPRESSANT MEDICATIONS

Depression with its patterned symptoms of moodiness, unhappiness, worry, and pessimism, is a major category of emotional illness in our society. Although amphetamines and other drugs have been used in treating depression, it was not until the late fifties that this category of medications came into its own. Since that time, numerous classes of antidepressants have been developed, all of which have their unique applications and contraindications.

MAJOR TYPES	Daily Dosages
Tricyclic	
1. Adapin/Sinequan (doxepin)	150–300mg
2. Anafranil (clomipramine)—new and still under investigation; must be obtained by contacting the manufacturer	
3. Aventyl/Pamelor (nortriptyline)	50–150mg
4. Elavinl/Endep (amitriptyline)	150–300mg
5. Norpramin/Pertofrane (desipramine)	150–300mg
6. Surmontil (trimipramine)	150–300mg
7. Tofranil/Janimine/Sk-Pramine (imipramine)	150–300mg
8. Tofranil/PM (imipramine pamoate)	150–300mg
9. Vivactil (protriptyline)	15–16mg
Tricyclic Combinations	
1. Triavil, etrafon (perphenazine-Amitriptyline HCI, MSD	
2. Deprol (meprobamate-benactyzine HCI)	
3. Limditrol (chlordiazepoxide-amitriptyline HCI)	
Other Antidepressants	
1. Ludiomil (maprotiline)	150–200mg
2. Asendin (amoxapine)	150–450mg
3. Desyrel (trazodone)	150–300mg
4. Prozac (fluoxetine)	20–80mg
New Antidepressants	
1. Wellbutrin (buproprion)	200–450mg
2. alprazolam (generic)	1.5–4.0mg
3. nomifensine (generic)	100–300mg
MAO Inhibitors	
1. Marplan (isocarboxazid)	30–50mg
2. Nardil (phenelzine)	45–90mg
3. Parnate (tranylcypromine)	30–50mg

Primary Uses

1. Indicated primarily in the treatment of depression, mood swings, sleep disorders, and anxiety.

Common Side Effects

1. Dry mouth, nasal congestion, constipation, difficulty with urination, tachycardia, and blurred vision
2. Lowered blood pressure and/or sedation
3. Dietary restrictions (marplan, nardil, parnate)-cheese, alcohol, chicken liver, yeast products, cream, pickled fish, chocolate, caffeine beverages, soy sauce, broad beans and certain other foods and drugs should be avoided.
4. Danger of death with overdose

Advocacy Tips

1. Uninformed mixing of these medications is dangerous
2. They typically take one-two weeks to begin to work
3. Abrupt withdrawal can create physical and emotional symptoms
4. Concurrent alcohol abuse is to be avoided
5. Should be used in conjunction with other causal intervention therapies when possible.

ANTIANXIETY MEDICATIONS

Anxiety is a common form of emotional distress. Symptoms include physical and emotional tension, inhibited self-confidence, withdrawal, sleep disruption, poor eating patterns, and phobias. This class of medications was established in the fifties, and has become one of the most widely distributed in this country.

MAJOR TYPES		DOSAGE RANGE
Benzodiazepines		
1.	Ativan/lorazepam	1–6mg
2.	Atarax,Vistaril/hydroxyzine	200–400mg
3.	Centrax, Verstran/prazepam	20–60mg
4.	Durrax/hydroxyzine	50–100mg
5.	Equanil, Miltown/meprobamate	1000–3000mg
6.	Librium/chlordiazepxide	15–40mg
7.	Paximpam/halasepam	60–160mg
8.	Serax/oxazepam	45–120mg
9.	Tranxene, Azene/chlorazepate	15–60mg
10.	Tybatran/tybamate	750–3000mg

11.	Valium/diazepam	5–40mg
12.	Xanax/alprazolam	1–4mg
Buspirone		
1.	BuSpar (buspirone HCI)	15–25mg
Meprobamates		
1.	Equanil, Miltown, Meprocon,	
2.	Meprospan, Neuramate, Neurate,	
3.	Sedabamate, Tranmep	1200–1600mg
Noradrenergic Agents		
1.	Catapres (clonidine)	1200–1600mg
2.	Inderal (propranolol)	60–160mg

Primary Uses

1. Relieves Anxiety
2. Relieves muscle tension
3. Sometimes used in alcohol detoxification
4. Insomnia

Common Side Effects

1. Strong potential for physical addiction
2. Drowsiness
3. Depression and impaired motor function
4. Withdrawal difficulties
5. High overdose potential
6. Paradoxical symptoms (opposite reaction)
7. Toxification danger—alcohol and other drugs
8. Dry mouth, blurred vision, and constipation

Advocacy Tips

1. Antianxiety medications should rarely be prescribed for more than 1–3 months.
2. Tolerance to these medications develops quickly.
3. Cojunctive therapy is recommended.
4. These medications should be discontinued slowly to avoid withdrawal.

ANTIPSYCHOTIC MEDICATIONS

Psychosis, potentially a highly debilitating disorder, is characterized by alterations in reality awareness, withdrawal, abnormal affect, and thought disruption. This class of drugs was also developed during the fifties and has had dramatic effects on those suffering from psychotic disorders, most especially schizophrenia.

MAJOR TYPES		DOSAGE RANGE
Phenothiazines		
1.	Compazine/prochlorperazine	50–75mg
2.	Quide/piperacetazine	20–160
3.	Mellaril/thiorodazine	50–600mg
4.	Proketazine/carphenazine	50–150mg
5.	Prolixin/fluphenazine	3–40mg
6.	Repoise/butaperazine	5–50mg
7.	Serentil/mesoridazine	25–200mg
8.	Sparine/promazine HCI	40–800mg
9.	Stelazine/trifluoperazine	4–40mg
10.	Thorazine/chlorpromazine	80–2000mg
11.	Tindal/acetophenazine	120–600mg
12.	Trilafon/perphenazine	12–64mg
13.	Vesprin/triflupromazine	150–500mg
Nonphenothiazines		
1.	Haldol/haloperidol	10–60mg
2.	Loxitane/loxapine	20–100mg
3.	Inapsine/droperidol (injection)	(by age)
4.	Moban/molindone	20–225mg
5.	Navane/thiothixine	6–60mg
6.	Orap/pimozide	3–20mg
7.	Serpasil/reserpine	.1–.25mg
8.	Taractan/chlorprothixene	20–200mg
9.	Tigan/trimethobenzamide	750–1000mg

Primary Uses

1. Relieve anxiety and agitation
2. Reduce unorganized thinking
3. Reduce hallucinations and delusions
4. Reduce paranoia

Common Side Effects

1. Sedation and/or lowered blood pressure
2. Extrapyramidal symptoms (EPS)—rigid walk, tongue chewing, generalized body movement dysfunction, flattened affect, excess rocking, pacing, etc.
3. Dry mouth, nasal congestion, and constipation
4. Impotence, sensitivity to sun, sensitivity to temperature extremes, and delayed menstruation

Advocacy Tips

1. Side effects are one of the major limitations of antipsychotic medications—artane, congentin, and benadryl are sometimes used to counter these effects
2. Long-term users of antipsychotic medications run a risk of permanent or fixed EPS, Tardive Dyskinesia and white blood cell loss
3. Mixing antipsychotic medications with other forms of medications should be done with caution
4. These drugs can create side effects in an unborn infant. Caution should be taken during pregnancy
5. Regular evaluation for Tardive Dyskinesia and white blood cell loss can help prevent serious or permanent damage

ANTIMANIC (MOOD STABILIZERS) MEDICATIONS

Lithium was approved for use in treating manic type illnesses in this country in the early seventies. It is a highly toxic drug, requiring substantial medical monitoring. Lithium's beneficial effects have been established; however the mechanism by which it works has not.

MAJOR TYPES		DOSAGES
1.	Lithonate, Eskalith, Lithane, Lithotabs, Lithobid (lithium carbonante)	600–2100mg
2.	Cibalith-S	5–10 ml qid
Other Mood Stabilizers		
1.	Depakene, Depakote (valproic acid)	200–1600mg

2. Klonapin/clonazepam 2–16mg
(used experimentally for acute mania)
3. Tegretol/carbomazepine 200–1200mg

Primary Uses

1. Used in control of manic behavior and bi-polar disorders
2. Used in mood stabilization and for control of violent episodes
3. Other uses for lithium are under investigation at this time

Common Side Effects

1. Nausea, diarrhea, tremors, tiredness, weight gain, and gastro distress
2. Toxicity is indicated by pronounced tremors, slurred speech and seizures.
3. Birth defects
4. Damage to thyroid and kidneys
5. Skin problems

Advocacy Tips

1. Lithium requires strict medical monitoring—there is a fine line between too much and too little.
2. Kidney functioning should be watched closely.
3. Diabetics should use Lithium with caution.
4. The need for careful diagnostic screening for manic type illness, physical evaluation, and constant monitoring should lead to selective utilization of this drug.

SEDATIVE MEDICATIONS

Sedatives are one of the oldest and largest classes of psychoactive medications. They have been used in low doses as a calming agent, moderate doses to induce sleep, and high doses as an anesthetic. Controls on these medications have increased in recent years due to their high abuse potential.

MAJOR TYPES	SLEEP INDUCING DOSE
Benzodiazepianes	
1. Ativan/lorazepam	2–4mg
2. Dalmane/flurazepam	15–30mg
3. Halcion/triazolam	.125–.5mg
4. Restoril/temazepam	15–30mg
Barbiturates	
1. Amytal/amobarbital	65–200mg
2. Atarate/aprobarbital	40–160mg
3. Bustisol/buticap (butibarbital)	50–100mg
4. Gemonil/metharbital	100mg
5. Lotusate/talbutal	120mg
6. Luminal/phenobarbital	100–320mg
7. Mebaral/mephobarbital	200mg
8. Nembual/pentobarbital	100–200mg
9. Seconal, Tuinal/secobarbital	50–200mg
Nonbarbiturates/Benzodiazepines	
1. Doriden/glutethimide	250–500mg
2. Noctec/chloral hydrate	500–1000mg
3. Nodular/methypryln	200–400mg
4. Placidyl/ethchlorvynol	500–750mg
5. Valmid/ethinamate	500–1000mg
Other medications used as sedatives	
1. Alcohol	*********

Primary Uses

1. Induce Sleep
2. Occasional use as an anesthetic
3. Some are used as antianxiety agents.

Common Side Effects

1. Drowsiness and lethargy
2. Skin rashes, nausea, vomiting
3. Paradoxical reaction in some individuals
4. Toxification danger when combined with other drugs

Advocacy Tips

1. This drug has extremely high abuse potential.
2. Quick tolerance development, dependence factor, and withdrawal complications are concerns.
3. This medication should be avoided during pregnancy.
4. Withdrawal after prolonged use (as little as two weeks) should be gradual—withdrawal syndrome is more serious than with opiates.

MISCELLANEOUS PSYCHOTHERAPEUTIC MEDICATIONS

The following are medications used in some psychotherapeutic applications.

STIMULANTS	APPLICATIONS
1. Amphetamines	Used in controlling narcolepsy and sometimes for appetite control
2. Caffeine	Increase alertness, appetite control
3. Ritalin, Cylert, Mazanor, Bontril, Tenuate, Anoxine	Treatment of hyperactivity in children

Concerns

1. Psychological addition with amphetamines
2. High abuse potential with amphetamines
3. Paradoxical reactions
4. May limit linear growth and weight
5. Research indicates that hyperactive children on these medications continue to experience school problems, behavior disorders, and self-concept disruption.
6. Use of these medications is not indicated without conjunctive intervention at home and school,—i.e., parent education and family therapy.

Antabuse/Disulfiram

Antabuse is used in the treatment of alcohol abuse. It discourages abuse by creating uncomfortable symptoms such as nausea, thirst, chest pain, palpitation, and breathing difficulty.

Concerns

1. In absence of alcohol, Antabuse can cause drowsiness, impotence, headache, aftertaste, and skin eruptions.
2. Can have a damaging effect on the liver
3. With alcohol abuse, can create shock and death
4. All forms of alcohol (foods, medicines, etc.) must be carefully avoided.
5. Should be used with caution with pregnancy, diabetes, epilepsy, brain damage, kidney disease, and heart disease.
6. This medication should be used only in conjunction with other therapies,—i.e., alcohol counseling.
7. Antabuse overdose can be catastrophic,—i.e., weeks of agitated psychosis.

CHAPTER 12

CONCLUSION

I appreciate the word *practical*, especially when that practicality has broad application. If I were an automobile engineer, I would much rather design a family sedan than a sports car. Both are fine and each has value, but the one that can be used by the most people for the most purposes captures my attention. I suppose that is why I felt the need to engineer **IntraActive Therapy**. I saw a need for a family sedan framework that would help the average therapist manage the mainstream of day-to-day problems.

I would be the first to admit that there is no special uniqueness or dynamic breakthrough inherent to **IntraActive Therapy**. Much of the information you have read has been shared, in differing forms, by others before me. What is special, however, is the way in which this approach is brought together. A disassembled automobile has little practical purpose until the parts are pulled into a workable whole. This is the value of **IntraActive Therapy**.

As you read this book, I am sure you noted the importance placed on **IntraActive Therapy** as a beginning. Take care that you treat what you have learned with this end in mind. **IntraActive Therapy** is attractive because it is simple, straightforward, and practical in application. In many ways it is like the foundation of a house. That foundation is a necessary beginning. What comes later is more diverse and complex, but equally important. I hope you will continue to build on your house, customizing it to your own specifications.

The development and culmination of this effort has been a demanding pleasure. It has helped me pull my thoughts and experiences together into a functional whole. I hope, in turn, that **IntraActive Therapy** will be of help to you in your own efforts. There is nothing that could mean more to me than to help the helpers.

APPENDIX A
PATIENT INTAKE INFORMATION

Name:	Date:
Address:	Physician(s):
Phone(s):	Referred by:

The following information will assist us in assessing your situation and determining how we may best be of help. We recognize this form as confidential information.

General Information

Birthplace ______________ Birthdate ______________ Age ________

Names & ages of children ______________________________

Present employment ______________________________

School and academic background ______________________________

Are you married, and if so, for how long? ______________________________

Health Status Information

Do you have any significant health difficulties? ______________________________

____

What medications, if any, are you currently taking? ______________________________

____

If you have received counseling/therapy before, please give us a brief summary of the reasons and outcome. ______________________________

____

____

Clinical Information

Are you having any of the following symptoms?

____ Depression	____ Nervousness	____ Sleeplessness
____ Low energy	____ Excessive anger	____ Unusual fears
____ Sexual problems	____ Marital Problems	____ Alcohol abuse
____ Drug abuse	____ Eating problems	____ Panic attacks
____ Moodiness	____ Memory loss	____ Chronic poor health
____ ____________	____ ____________	____ ____________

Problem Assessment

Please give us a brief summary of why you came for assistance.

____

____

____

Our standard therapy fee is $____ per session (approximately 50 minutes.) In most cases, patients are seen on a once-a-week basis for an average of 6–8 sessions. Unless special arrangements are made, your charges are due at the completion of each visit.

________ I will pay my charges as I go.
________ I would like to pay my balance in full at the end of the month. My reasons are ____
________ I would like to discuss other options.

Date: ____________________ Signed: ____________________

Please note that your charges must be handled as indicated above. If you have an exceptional need, please discuss this with your therapist. Collection charges and legal fees will be charged to your account.

In most cases, your medical insurance will cover a portion of your therapy charges. You will be given a receipt following each visit and a monthly statement on request. Either contains the information and codes necessary for you to submit your claim for reimbursement through your insurance company. Please let us know if you require additional information or assistance. Due to the variance in medical insurance coverage policies, we can assume no responsibility for your company's coverage of our services.

PATIENT INFORMATION RELEASE

I, ______________________________, do hereby freely agree to allow my therapist to discuss relevant aspects of my (or my child's) treatment with my physician, or other appropriate individuals, as it relates to facilitating an appropriate treatment process. This release of information will occur only in strictest confidence and discretion by my therapist.

Please note that we are legally required to report child sexual abuse information or threats that involve danger to others.

Date: Signed:

____________________ ____________________

APPENDIX B.
SENTENCE COMPLETION INVENTORY

Name: Date:
Age: Sex:

This inventory is designed as a subjective and basic tool for identifying certain personal characteristics. Please be as open and honest as possible as you complete the following sentences. This is not a researched measuring instrument.

_____ 1. I feel comfortable ______________________.
_____ 2. I would like to be ______________________.
_____ 3. Most people think I ______________________.
_____ 4. I get tired ______________________.
_____ 5. My least favorite emotion is ______________________.
_____ 6. I sleep ______________________.
_____ 7. My childhood was ______________________.
_____ 8. I feel nervous ______________________.
_____ 9. My eating habits are ______________________.
_____ 10. In my life, stability is ______________________.
_____ 11. Our society is ______________________.
_____ 12. My appearance is ______________________.
_____ 13. I just hate to ______________________.
_____ 14. The place I live is ______________________.
_____ 15. As a person, I believe I am ______________________.
_____ 16. With others, one must be ______________________.
_____ 17. I enjoy ______________________.
_____ 18. For me, exercise is ______________________.
_____ 19. If I could change me, I would change ______________________.
_____ 20. When life throws me curves, I ______________________.
_____ 21. Regarding good and bad, I must notice ______________________.
_____ 22. I am sick ______________________.
_____ 23. My work life is ______________________.
_____ 24. My family treats me ______________________.
_____ 25. For the most part, life is ______________________.

Health	Security	Image	Relations	Awareness	
4 ( )	1 ( )	2 ( )	3 ( )	5 ( )	0 = negative
6 ( )	10( )	8 ( )	7 ( )	13( )	1 = neutral
9 ( )	14( )	12( )	11( )	17( )	2 = positive
18( )	20( )	15( )	16( )	21( )	
22( )	23( )	19( )	24( )	25( )	
____	____	____	____	____	

Rate each answer as a negative, neutral, or positive response and assign value. Add response values above for respective questions. A low score (under 4) indicates area of concern.

APPENDIX C. THE INTRAACTIVE PSYCHOLOGICAL INVENTORY (IPI) (EXPERIMENTAL VERSION) CARL MUMPOWER, PH.D.

Information & Utilization of the IPI

Uses and Purposes

The IPI is a brief inventory that is useful in assessing 10 identified areas significant to psychological health. These categories represent the more common areas of psychological dysfunction, and can help target therapeutic intervention efforts.

Clinical Utilization

The IPI is a simple self-report inventory. No research has been done on its reliability or validity. It should be used only as a general guide for identifying individual problem areas.

Assessment Areas

One—**Anxiety**

Assesses general level of anxiety and emotional insecurity. A high score (7–10) indicates an extreme anxiety level that may include panic attacks. A low score (0–3) indicates minimal emotional insecurity.

Two—**Depression**

Assesses mood level. A high score indicates chronic or intense depression, while a low score marks a normal and limited type of depressive symptoms.

Three—**Fragmentation**

Assesses conceptual abilities and reality awareness. A high score is indicative of fragmented thought patterns and psychosis of some form. A low score indicates a normal level of functioning in this area.

Four—**Identity confusion**

Assesses ego function and integration. A high score is indicative of severe identity disruption and borderline functioning. A low score indicates a normal identity formation.

Five—**Antisocial attitudes**

Assesses level of psychopathology. A high score indicates severe psychopathic attitudes, while a low score indicates minimal dysfunction in this area.

Six—**Somatic concerns**

Assesses somatic tendencies. A high score indicates multiple physical complaints and concerns. A low score indicates limited somatic issues.

Seven—**Paranoia**

Assesses level of paranoid ideation. A high score indicates multiple paranoid perceptions and concerns. A low score is indicative of more normalized perceptions.

Eight—**Manic behaviors**

Assesses existence of manic behavior patterns. A high score indicates pervasive or repetitive manic episodes. A low score indicates a normal level of excitability.

Nine—**Obsession and Compulsivity**

Assesses level of obsessive thought and/or compulsive behavior. A high score indicates intrusive levels of obsession and/or compulsivity. A low score indicates normal functioning in this area.

Ten—**Substances**

Assesses perceived level of substance use. A high score indicates pervasive substance use and symptoms. A low score indicates a nondisruptive or minimal substance use pattern.

Scoring and Interpreting the IPI

There are 10 questions for each of 10 areas. The questions are arranged so that all that end in 1 address area one, all that end in 2 address area two and so forth. To score the IPI begin with the first area and count all of the true responses in the upper two sections and all the false responses in the lower two sections. The combined values of these responses equals the respondents corresponding score in the respective area.

INTRAACTIVE PSYCHOLOGICAL INVENTORY (EXPERIMENTAL VERSION) BY DR. CARL MUMPOWER

Directions —Using the separate answer sheet, circle the most correct response to the following true-false questions. This is not a test of your abilities. If you respond honestly and openly, you will obtain more accurate results. Base your answers on the way you are versus the way you used to be or would like to be.

1. Sometimes I feel nervous.
2. I feel sad on occasion.

3. I think a lot.
4. I feel unsure of myself sometimes.
5. I sometimes get in trouble.
6. I am sick a bit too often.
7. There's been some hurt in my life.
8. My moods go up and down.
9. I try to do things well.
10. I use alcohol or drugs recreationally.
11. New situations are rarely uncomfortable.
12. I seldom wake up feeling sad.
13. I keep my thinking under control.
14. I am confident in who I am.
15. I need people in my life.
16. I don't get sick much.
17. People generally understand me.
18. I appear relaxed to other people.
19. I don't worry too much about details.
20. I never use drugs or alcohol.
21. Sometimes my hands shake from stress.
22. I feel down more than I should.
23. I am confused a lot.
24. I feel uncertain about myself.
25. I believe most people are dishonest.
26. I have lots of aches and pains.
27. I get afraid at night.
28. I need little sleep for days at a time.
29. I am a bit of a perfectionist.
30. Drinking helps me relax.
31. I was rarely nervous as a child.
32. I am not sad very often.
33. I think pretty clearly.
34. I have few doubts about myself.
35. I love a good number of people.
36. I can think myself out of being tired.

37. I have no problem being trusting.
38. My behavior doesn't tend to go up and down.
39. Disorganization doesn't bother me much.
40. Getting high isn't important to me.
41. Crowds make me feel uncomfortable.
42. I worry more than I should.
43. Sometimes my mind seems out of control.
44. I often wish I was someone else.
45. I get most people before they get me.
46. My moods affect my health.
47. I live in fear of being hurt.
48. My mind seomtimes feels like a runaway train.
49. Sometimes I worry too much about little things.
50. I come from a family who misused alcohol or drugs.
51. My nerves rarely make me withdraw.
52. I am not one to feel down very much.
53. I have no trouble understanding things.
54. I keep my feelings private.
55. Relationships are important to me.
56. I rarely make complaints about my health.
57. I don't worry much about what others think.
58. I have fairly good control over my moods.
59. I feel it is OK to make mistakes.
60. Most of my friends aren't much into getting high.
61. I feel jittery inside quite often.
62. I feel tired a lot.
63. My mind seems out of control.
64. I wish I understood myself more.
65. It's a dog eat dog world out there.
66. I feel tired and sick a lot.
67. Others think I am overly suspicious.
68. People tell me I am too hyper.
69. I do things until I get them right.
70. I've had legal or job problems over alcohol.

71. I seldom feel insecure.
72. I feel sad very infrequently.
73. I don't feel dominated by thoughts.
74. I do as well as everyone else.
75. I rarely use drugs or drink.
76. I enjoy good health most of the time.
77. I feel relaxed and comfortable with people.
78. My behavior is not usually inconsistent.
79. I worry about things very little.
80. I don't need a high to ease my worries.
81. Sometimes I feel scared of everything.
82. I get so down I feel I can't go on.
83. I wonder if I am going crazy.
84. I have a fear of confident people.
85. I am able to fool people a lot.
86. I worry that my health is getting worse.
87. I think that someone is going to get me.
88. When I am up, I am really up.
89. I never feel like I do things good enough.
90. I get high enough to effect my health.
91. I never have panic attacks.
92. I don't think much about suicide.
93. I don't believe I have crazy thoughts.
94. I know who I am.
95. I cry and feel pain like most people do.
96. I am proud of my good health.
97. I get along well with difficult people.
98. I stay on an even keel most of time.
99. I am rarely disorganized.
100. I do not need to get high to feel OK.

The IntraActive Psychological Inventory (IPI)
By Dr. Carl Mumpower

Answer Sheet

1.	T	F	21.	T	F	41.	T	F	61.	T	F	81.	T	F
2.	T	F	22.	T	F	42.	T	F	62.	T	F	82.	T	F
3.	T	F	23.	T	F	43.	T	F	63.	T	F	83.	T	F
4.	T	F	24.	T	F	44.	T	F	64.	T	F	84.	T	F
5.	T	F	25.	T	F	45.	T	F	65.	T	F	85.	T	F
6.	T	F	26.	T	F	46.	T	F	66.	T	F	86.	T	F
7.	T	F	27.	T	F	47.	T	F	67.	T	F	87.	T	F
8.	T	F	28.	T	F	48.	T	F	68.	T	F	88.	T	F
9.	T	F	29.	T	F	49.	T	F	69.	T	F	89.	T	F
10.	T	F	30.	T	F	50.	T	F	70.	T	F	90.	T	F
11.	T	F	31.	T	F	51.	T	F	71.	T	F	91.	T	F
12.	T	F	32.	T	F	52.	T	F	72.	T	F	92.	T	F
13.	T	F	33.	T	F	53.	T	F	73.	T	F	93.	T	F
14.	T	F	34.	T	F	54.	T	F	74.	T	F	94.	T	F
15.	T	F	35.	T	F	55.	T	F	75.	T	F	95.	T	F
16.	T	F	36.	T	F	56.	T	F	76.	T	F	96.	T	F
17.	T	F	37.	T	F	57.	T	F	77.	T	F	97.	T	F
18.	T	F	38.	T	F	58.	T	F	78.	T	F	98.	T	F
19.	T	F	39.	T	F	59.	T	F	79.	T	F	99.	T	F
20.	T	F	40.	T	F	60.	T	F	80.	T	F	100.	T	F

____	____	____	____	____	____	____	____	____	____
Anx	Dep	Fra	Idt	Ant	Som	Par	Man	Obs	Sub

APPENDIX D.
RECOMMENDED READINGS

Adult Children of Alcoholics: Janet G. Woititx. Health Communications, Inc., Deerfield Beach, Florida, 1983.

Anxiety and Panic Attacks, Their Cause and Cure: Robert Handley. Fawcett-Crest Inc., New York, 1985.

Codependent No More: Melody Beattie. Harper & Row, New York, 1987.

Feeling Good-The New Mood Therapy: David D. Burns. Penguin Books, U.S.A., 1980.

Games People Play: Eric Burns. Ballantine Publishers. New York, 1964.

Good Behavior: Stephen W. Garber, Marianne D. Garber, and Robyn F. Spizman. Villard Books, New York, 1987.

Hazards of Being Male: Herb Goldberg. Signet Publishers, New York, 1976.

Healing the Child Within: Charles L. Whitfield. Health Communications, Deerfield Beach, Florida, 1989.

How To Be an Assertive (Not Aggressive) Women: Jean Bair. Penguin Books, New York, 1976.

How To Live With Your Teenager: Peter H. Buntman, Eleanor M. Saris. Ballantine Books, New York, 1979.

How To Raise Your Self-Esteem: Nathaniel Brandon. Bantam Books, New York, 1987.

How To Win Friends and Influence People: Dale Carnegie. Pocket Books, New York, 1936.

I'm O.K.—You're O.K.: Thomas Harris. Avon Books, New York, 1967.

Living, Loving, and Learning: Leo Buscaglia. Fawcett-Crest Inc., New York, 1982.

Love: Leo Buscaglia. Fawcett-Crest Inc., New York, 1972.

Love is Letting Go of Fear: Gerald Jampolsky. Celestrial Arts, Berkeley, California, 1979.

Men are Just Desserts: Sonya Friedman. Warner Books, New York, 1983.

Necessary Loses: Judith Viorst. Fawcett-Crest Inc., New York, 1986.

Passages: Gail Sheehy. Bantam Books, New York, 1976.

Positive Addiction: W. Glasser. Harper & Row, New York, 1976.

Pulling Your Own Strings: Wayne W. Dyer. Avon Books, New York, 1978.

Reality Therapy: Glasser. Perennial Publishers, New York, 1964.

Recovery: A Guide For Adult Children of Alcoholics: Herbert Gravitz and Julie Bowden. Simon and Schuster Publishing Co., New York, 1985.

Strengthening Your Step-family: E. Einstein & L. Albert. American Guidance Service, Circle Pines, Minnesota, 1986.

The Dance of Anger: Harriet Goldher Lerner. Harper & Row, New York, 1985.
The Dance of Intimacy: Harriet Goldher Lerner. Harper & Row, New York, 1989.
The Road Less Traveled: Scott Peck. Simon and Schuster Publishing Co., New York, 1978.
Tough Love: P. York, D. York, and T. Watchel. Bantam Books, New York, 1982.
Toxic Parents: Susan Forward. Bantam Books, New York, 1989.
Women Who Love Men Too Much: Robin Norwood. Pocket Books, New York, 1985.
Your Erroneous Zones: Wayne Dyer. Avon Books, New York, 1976.

BIBLIOGRAPHY

Adler, Alfred: The Individual Psychology of Alfred Adler. Harper & Row, New York, 1956.
Alberti, Robert, and Emmons, Micheal: Your Perfect Right. Impact Press, San Luis Obispo, California, 1982.
Allport, Gorden: The Person in Psychology. Beacon Press, Boston, 1968.
Ayd, Frank: Rational Psychopharmacotherapy and the Right to Treatment. Ayd Medical Communications, Baltimore, Maryland, 1975.
Bandura, A.: Behavioral Modification Through Modeling Procedures. Holt, Reinhart, and Winston Publishing Co., New York, 1965.
Barten, H.: Brief Therapies. Behavioral Publications, New York, 1971.
Beck, Aaron: Depression: Clinical, Experimental, and Theoretical Aspects. Harper & Row, New York, 1967.
Bergman, Joel: Fishing For Barracuda: The Pragmatics of Brief Systematic Therapy. W. W. Norton & Co., New York, 1985.
Bowen, Murray: Family Therapy In Clinical Practice. Jason Aronson, Inc., New York, 1978.
Carnegie, Dale: How To Win Friends and Influence People. Pocket Books, New York, 1936.
Collier, Helen: Counseling Women. A Division of Macmillan Publications Co., Inc., New York, 1982.
Ellis, Albert, and Grieger, Russell: Handbook of Rational Emotive Therapy. Springer Publishing Co., New York, 1977.
Erickson, E. H.: Identity: Youth and Crisis. W. W. Norton and Co., New York, 1968.
Fagan, J., and Shepherd I.: Gestalt Therapy Now. Science and Behavior Books, Inc., Palo Alto, California, 1970.
Fine, Reuben: Troubled Men. Jossey-Bass Publishers, San Francisco, 1988.
Franks, Violet, and Rothblum, Esther: The Stereotyping of Women. Springer Publishing Co., New York, 1983.
Freud, Anna: The Ego and the Mechanisms of Defense. The Hozarth Press and The Institute of Psychoanalysis, London, 1961.
Glasser, William: Reality Therapy. Harper & Row, New York, 1965.
Griest, J., Jefferson, J., and Marks, I.: Anxiety and Its Treatment. Warner Books, New York, 1986.
Gustafson, James: The Complex Secrets of Brief Psychotherapy. W. W. Norton and Co., New York, 1986.
Harris, Thomas: I'm O.K.—You're O.K. Harper & Row Publishing Co., New York, 1967.

James, William: The Principles of Psychology, Volume I and II: Henry Holt and Co., New York, 1908.

Johnson, V.: I'll Quit Tomorrow. Harper & Row, San Francisco, 1980.

Kadis, Asya, Kresner, Jack, Weiner, Myron, Winick, Charles, and Foulkes, S.: Practicum of Group Psychotherapy, Harper and Row, 1974.

Kline, Paul: Fact and Fantasy in Freudian Theory: Methuen and Co., London, 1972.

Lader, Malcolm: The Psychophysiology of Mental Illness. Routledge and Kegan Paul Ltd., Boston, 1975.

Lewis, Jerry: Swimming Upstream: Teaching and Learning Psychotherapy in a Biological Era. Brunner/Mazel Inc., New York, 1991.

Loew, Clemons, and Grayson, Henry, and Loew, Gloria: Three Psychotherapies. Brunner/Magel Inc., New York, 1975.

May, Rollo: The Courage to Create. Bantam Books, New York, 1975.

Malan, David: The Frontier of Brief Psychotherapy. Plenum Publishing, New York, 1971.

Mering, Otto, and King, Stanley: Remotivating the Mental Patient. Russell Sage Foundation, New York, 1957.

Minuchin, Salvador: Families and Family Therapy. Harvard University Press, Cambridge, Massachusetts, 1974.

Morawetz, Anita, and Walker, Gillian: Brief Therapy With Single Parented Families. Brunner/Magel Inc., New York,

Moustakas, Clark: Loneliness & Love. Prentice Hall, Englewood Cliffs, New Jersey, 1974.

Patterson, C.: Theories of Counseling and Psychotherapy. Harper & Row Publishing Co., New York, 1966.

Peck, Scott: People of The Lie, The Hope for Healing, Human Evil. Simon and Schuster, Inc., New York, 1983.

Perls, Frederick: Gestalt Therapy Verbatim. Bantam Books, Inc., NY, 1969.

Phillips, Lakin, and Wiener, David: Short Term Psychotherapy and Structured Behavior Changes, McGraw-Hill, Inc. New York, 1966.

Pittenger, Robert, Hockett, Charles, and Danky, John: The First Five Minutes. Paul Martineacu Publishing Co., Ithaca, New York, 1960.

Polansky, Norman: Ego Psychology and Communication. Atherton Press, New York, 1971.

Rabkin, Richard: Strategic Psychotherapy. Basic Books, New York, 1977.

Rachman, S., and Maser, J.: Panic. Laurance Erlbaum Associates, Hillsdale, New Jersey, 1988.

Rank, Otto: Will Therapy, Truth, and Reality. Alfred A. Knoff, Inc., New York, 1945.

Rogers, Carl: Client Centered Therapy, Houghton-Mifflin Co., Boston, 1951.
Sifneos, P.: Short-term Psychotherapy and Emotional Crisis. Harvard University Press, Cambridge, Massachusetts, 1972.
Sonnenberg, Stephen, Blank, Arthur, and Talbott: The Trauma of War: Stress and Recovery in Vietnam Veterans, American Psychiatric Press, Washington, 1985.
Vistosky, Harold: Courage, Creativity and Cost-effectiveness: The challenge for a Psychiatric Program Administrator, Administrative Issues in Public Mental Health. Jossey-Bass, Inc., San Francisco, 1991.
Wedding, Danny, Horton, Arthur, and Webster, Jeffrey: The Neuropsychology Handbook. Springer Publishing Co., New York, 1986.
White, Marjorie, and Weiner, Marcella: The theory and Practice of Self Psychology. Brummer/Mazel Publishers, New York, 1986.
Widom, Cathy: Sex Roles and Psychopathology. Plenum Press, New York, 1984.
Wirken, Georgia: Quick Fixes and Small Comforts. Villard Books, New York, 1988.
Wolpe, Joseph: The Practice of Behavior Therapy. Pergamon Press, Inc., Elmsford, New York, 1990.
Wolff, Sula: Childhood and Human Nature. Routledge, New York, 1989.

DRUG REFERENCE BIBLIOGRAPHY

Abrams, Anne C.: Clinical Drug Therapy. J. B. Lippincott Co., Philadelphia, 1987.

Baer, Charold C., and Williams, Bradley R.: Clinical Pharmacology & Nursing. Springhouse Corporation, Springhouse, Pennsylvania, 1988.

Clayton, Bruce D.: Mosby's Handbook of Pharmacology. C. V. Mosby Co., St. Louis, Illinois, 1987.

DeBenedetto, Frank E.: The Family Physician's Compendium of Drug Therapy. McGraw-Hill, Inc., New York, 1989.

Dubousky, Stephen C. and Weissburg, Micheal P.: Clinical Psychology in Primary Care. Waverly Press, Inc., Baltimore, Maryland, 1983.

Faumand, Beverly J. and Faumand, Micheal, P.: Emergency Psychiatry for the House Officer. Waverly Press, Inc., Baltimore, Maryland, 1983.

Goode, E.: Drugs in Modern Society (2nd ed.). Random House, New York, 1984.

Grilly, D.: Drugs and Human Behavior. Allyn & Bacon, Needham, Massachusetts, 1989.

Harkness, Richard: OTC Handbook. Medical Economics Co., Oradell, New Jersey, 1978.

Physicians Desk Reference for Non-Prescriptive Drugs. Medical Economics Co., Oradell, New Jersey, 1989.

Schalzburg, A. F. and Cole, J. O.: Manuel of Clinical Pharmacology (6th ed.). American Psychiatric Press, Washington, D.C., 1986.

Simon, E.: Drugs in Modern Society (2nd ed.). Random House, New York, 1984.

INDEX

Acetophenazine, 123
Adapt, 7, 14, 63, 66, 76, 78, 106
Addictive, 29, 53, 69, 80, 81
Adler, Alfred, 11, 38
Adversity, 79
Advising, 88
Affairs, 82
Affection, 10, 51, 68, 102
Agenda, 32, 55, 107
Agoraphobia, 34
Alberti, Robert, et al., 80
Alcohol, 36, 121, 122, 126–28
Alcohol detoxification, 122
Alcoholics, 103
Allport, Gordon, 1, 46, 50, 59, 70
Alprazolam, 122
Amitriptyline, 120
Amobarbital, 126
Amoxapine, 120
Amphetamines, 127
Amytal, 126
Anger, 35, 39, 66, 71, 79, 110, 114, 116
Anoxine, 127
Antabuse, 127, 128
Antidepressants, 120
Anxiety, 5, 25, 31, 77, 81, 114, 120–23
Apprehension, 58, 90, 104, 105
Aprobarbital, 126
Artane, 124
Asendin, 120
Atarate, 126
Atarax, 121
Ativan, 121, 126
Attention, 20, 23, 28, 31, 51, 60, 68, 82, 102, 109, 113, 129
Autonomy, 62, 90
Availability, 7, 44, 47, 90, 91, 96, 119
Aventyl, 120
Avoidance, 30, 34, 45, 61, 67, 102
Ayd, Frank, 46
Azene, 121

Balance, 13, 27–29, 36, 81, 94, 95, 98, 103
Bandura, A., 51
Barbiturates, 126
Barten, H., 2, 26
Beck, Aaron, 28
Benadryl, 124
Benzodiazepianes, 126
Benzodiazepines, 121, 126
Bergman, Joel, 13, 50
Bonded, 56, 63
Bontril, 127
Boundaries, 20, 21, 55, 91–93
Bowen, Murray, 21, 44
BuSpar, 122
Buspirone, 122

Bustisol, 126
Butaperazine, 123
Buticap, 126

Caffeine, 121, 127
Candor, 50, 51, 58
Carbomazepine, 125
Care, 2, 6, 10, 19, 21, 28, 46, 51, 70, 89, 93, 94, 97, 98, 101, 104, 106, 129
Careers, 22
Carnegie, Dale, 37
Carphenazine, 123
Catapres, 122
Catharsis, 39, 41
Centrax, 121
Change, 1, 3, 6, 7, 9, 26, 27, 33–35, 37, 44–47, 53–56, 59–61, 66, 70, 71, 74–79, 84, 86–88, 90, 94, 96, 100, 103, 105, 109–13, 115
Checklists, 18
Children, working with, 101
Chloral hydrate, 126
Chlordiazepxide, 121
Chlorpromazine, 123
Chlorprothixene, 123
Cibalith-S, 124
Clients, working with difficult, 102
Clonazepam, 125
Coasting, 6, 77, 78
Co-dependent people, 103
Collier, Helen, 79
Colors, 106
Commitment, 52
Compassion, 6, 91
Competition and professional conflict, 97
Confidentiality, 89
Conflict, 24, 50, 66, 73, 79, 80, 95, 97, 100, 109
Conflicts, 24
Contraindications, 120
Control, 13, 14, 16, 29, 30, 36, 37, 44, 47, 71, 73, 76, 78, 79, 87, 97, 99, 105, 107, 110, 113, 115, 116, 125, 127
Control, internal, 13, 14, 30, 38, 54, 74
Courage, 6, 15, 71, 87, 97, 98
Counseling setting, your, 105, 106
Creativity, 62, 63
Credentials, 58, 91, 101, 106
Credibility, 51, 88, 91
Cylert, 127

Dalmane, 126
Danger, 53, 109, 121, 122, 126
Data, biographical, 18, 89
Death, 128
Defenses, 6, 61, 65–68, 70, 71, 74, 83, 102, 103
Delusions, 123
Denial, 30, 67, 102
Depakene, 124
Depakote, 124
Dependency, 60, 61
Depression, 31, 32, 77, 119, 122
Depression, recurring, 25
Desipramine, 120
Desyrel, 120
Development, 1, 10, 38, 57, 71, 84, 85, 87, 90, 91, 93, 96, 127, 129
Diarrhea, 125
Diazepam, 122
Direction, 10, 15, 16, 19, 35, 37, 38, 50, 55, 58, 60, 61, 69, 70, 73, 77, 87, 88, 103, 106, 109
Dishonesty, 53, 66, 92, 102
Disorders, character, 75, 103
Disorders, phobic, 25
Disorders, psychosomatic, 25
Disorders, sleep, 120
Distraction, 36, 67, 69, 80
Do, 27, 33
Documentation, 93, 94

Doexpin, 120
Doriden, 126
Dreaming, 37
Droperidol, 123
Drugs, 122, 126
Durrax, 121
Dysfunction, 25, 26, 71
Dysfunctional exposure, 83

Education and training, continuing, 96
Elavil, 120
Ellis, Albert, et al., 76
Emotional catharsis, 39, 41, 42
Emotional stability, 13
Employer, 89
Endure, 52, 78, 82, 97
Energy, 6, 28, 35, 36, 50, 53, 55, 59, 75, 77, 86, 96–98, 101, 103, 109, 110
Energy and consistency, 98
Entrenchment, 71
Equanil, 121, 122
Erickson, Erik, 10, 12
Escape, 32, 68, 69, 108
Eskalith, 124
Ethchlorvynol, 126
Ethical, 55, 92, 105, 107
Ethinamate, 126
Expectations, 46, 58
Experience, 1–3,10, 24, 25, 28, 30, 32, 34, 38, 41, 42, 58, 62, 66, 68, 76, 77, 82, 84, 85, 98, 100–2, 107, 108, 110, 111, 113, 118, 127
External control, 13–15, 30, 36, 38, 39, 47, 103

Fading, 62–64
Fagan, J., et al., 13, 33
Failings, 11
Faith, 20, 51, 52, 67, 77, 92, 116
Families, 14, 21, 81, 82, 84, 100
Family, 10, 14, 18, 19, 21, 43, 44, 68, 85, 98–101, 103, 107, 112, 113, 116–18, 127, 129
Family members, 21, 99, 100
Fantasy, 30, 50, 67
Fear, 13, 15, 16, 34, 36, 40, 71, 84, 87, 102, 104, 105, 114
Feel, 7, 9, 18–21, 27, 29–34, 37–40, 51–55, 66, 70, 71, 74, 78, 79, 82, 85, 88, 90, 93, 97, 98, 102, 104, 106–8, 111, 112, 114, 116–18
Fees, 94, 95
Fine, Reuben, 73, 78, 125, 129
Flexibility, 7, 15, 66, 72, 99, 101
Flexible, 26, 43, 92
Fluphenazine, 123
Flurazepam, 126
Focus, 7, 10, 19, 22, 24, 27, 28, 35, 37, 38, 43, 50, 54, 55, 70, 80, 84, 92, 100, 109, 110
Formation, 9, 12, 75
Formative years, 11, 71
Franks, Violet, et al., 78
Feeling, free, 39–41
Freud, Anna, 40, 66–68, 72
Freud, Sigmund, 40
Fun, 50, 66, 102, 110
Future, 2, 9–13, 15, 16, 19, 25, 30, 70, 71, 73, 116

Gemonil, 126
Glasser, William, 10–12, 15, 20, 47, 50, 51, 62, 76, 83
Glutethimide, 126
Goal setting, 33, 35
Goals, 16, 35, 54, 55, 61, 86, 92, 100, 110
Griest, J., et al., 41
Groups, working with, 108
Growth, 11, 33, 35, 38, 47, 55–57, 60, 61, 75, 86, 90, 98, 104, 105, 116, 127
Guidance, 10, 11, 75

Guilt, 86, 114
Gustafason, James, 18, 57, 62, 63, 71

Halasepam, 121
Halcion, 126
Haldol, 123
Haloperidol, 123
Happiness, 13, 16, 78, 83
Harris, Thomas, 74
History, 17–19, 35, 110
Hobby, 98
Honest, 53, 92, 104, 111
Honesty, 18, 52, 53, 89, 91, 114
Hope, 6, 7, 15, 16, 34, 59, 63, 84, 86, 101, 112, 129
Humor, 99, 109
Hurts, 14, 78, 86
Hydroxyzine, 121

Identity, 9, 12, 13, 19, 25, 61, 64–66, 69, 73–75, 80–83, 103, 107
Imipramine, 120
Imposter syndrome, 98
Impression, clinical, 17, 23, 107
Inapsine, 123
Inconsistencies, 22, 59, 70, 72
Independent, 28, 62, 73
Inderal, 122
Individual, assessing the, 17
Insecure, 97
Insecurity, 73, 97, 106
Insomnia, 122
Instinct, 23, 72
Insurance, 44, 104
Insurance, liability, 104
Intelligence, 22, 70
Intensity, 25, 63, 67, 74, 84, 102, 109, 110
Intentionally, 12, 23, 39, 61, 63
Intervention, 1–4, 24–26, 39, 43, 45, 48, 49, 57, 60, 61, 75, 84, 105, 121, 127
Intervention methods, 2, 24, 25, 43
Intervention phase, 60, 61
Interventions, secondary, 45
Interviewing, 20
Inventories, informal, 18, 21, 22
Isocarboxazid, 120
Isolation, 67, 98

James, William, 1
Johnson, V., 81
Judge, 40, 86, 106, 110
Judgment errors and mistakes, 105

Kadis, Asya, et al., 71
Kline, Paul, 40
Klonapin, 125
Knowledge, 1, 5, 6, 12, 23, 28, 46, 63, 76, 87, 91, 93, 96, 100, 109

Lader, Malcolm, 80
Learning disabilities, 11, 14, 22, 28, 93, 96, 113, 116, 118
Legal considerations, 104
Lewis, Jerry, 1, 12, 46
Liabilities, 71
Librium, 121
Licensure, 91, 96
Lifestyle, 10, 31, 73, 77, 114
Limitations, 2, 4, 5, 19, 23, 44, 50, 90–92, 95, 124
Listening, 59, 88
Lithane, 124
Lithobid, 124
Lithonate, 124
Lithotabs, 124
Living, 14, 15, 23, 28, 30–32, 35, 39, 52, 53, 66, 69, 70, 77, 79–82, 94, 97, 117, 118
Loneliness, 14, 99
Lorazepam, 121, 126
Lotusate, 126
Love, 10, 11, 14, 32, 38, 50, 65, 67, 68, 73, 75, 78, 79, 82, 92, 98, 101, 102, 116

Loew, Clemmons, et al., 50
Loxapine, 123
Loxitane, 123
Ludiomil, 120
Luminal, 126

Malan, David, 2
Man, macho, 72, 73
Man, meek, 72, 73
Man, mature, 73
MAO inhibitors, 120
Maprotiline, 120
Marplan, 120, 121
Marriage, 56, 100, 115, 117
Mate, 78, 79
Maturity, 15, 55, 75, 88, 108
May, Rollo, 38, 63
Mazanor, 127
Mebaral, 126
Mellaril, 123
Mephobarbital, 126
Meprobamates, 122
Meprocon, 122
Meprospan, 122
Mering, Otto, et al., 11
Mesoridazine, 123
Metharbital, 126
Methodologies, 2, 5, 96
Methypryln, 126
Miltown, 121, 122
Minuchin, Salvador, 11, 14, 21
Mistakes, 31, 39, 54, 86, 105, 110, 116
Moban, 123
Model, 1, 2, 10, 20, 30, 49–51, 81, 85, 93, 107, 109, 116
Models, 1, 2, 10, 11, 14, 19, 21, 33, 44, 73, 74, 79, 84, 116
Molindone, 123
Monoamine oxidase inhibitors, 120
Mood stabilizers, 124
Morawetz, Anita, et al., 14
Moustasas, Clark, 51
Myopic, 4, 28, 99, 109
Myths, 2

Narcolepsy, 127
Nardil, 120, 121
Nausea, 125–27
Navane, 123
Nembual, 126
Neurate, 122
Neurotic, 100
Noctec, 126
Nodular, 126
Nonjudgmental, 18
Nonphenothiazines, 123
Noradrenergic Agents, 122
Norpramine, 120
Nortriptyline, 120
Nurturing, 12, 14, 40, 40, 79, 86

Obsession, 29, 36, 67
Obsessive, 29, 32, 37
Openness, 20, 52, 53, 58, 89
Orap, 123
Oxazepam, 121

Pain, 6, 10, 25, 32, 39–41, 53, 54, 59, 66–68, 71, 77, 82, 84, 86, 96, 99, 127
Pamelor, 120
Paradoxical reaction, 126
Paralysis, behavioral, 33, 34
Paranoid, 26, 102
Parent, 18, 50, 89, 101, 127
Parents, 9–12, 19, 21, 50, 82, 85, 101, 117, 118
Parnate, 120, 121
Passion, 7, 110
Past, 2, 9–13, 19, 25, 54, 60, 71, 83, 85, 86, 103, 114–16
Pathological, 24, 25, 76
Pathological problems, 25
Patience, 50, 68, 74, 75, 84, 102, 110
Patterning, 72

Patterson, C., 22
Paximpam, 121
Peck, Scott, 74, 83
Pecking order, 97
Peers, 11, 12, 90, 97, 109
Pentobarbital, 126
Perceptiveness, 7
Perls, Frederick, 13
Perphenazine, 123
Personality tests, 22
Personalization, 45, 47, 93, 106
Phenelzine, 120
Phenobarbital, 126
Phenothiazines, 123
Phillips, Lakin, et al., 15, 16, 34
Physical, 2, 11, 19, 24–25, 75, 80–81, 92, 105–6, 113–14, 117, 121–22, 125
Physicians, 95
Pimozode, 123
Piperacetazine, 123
Pittenger, Robert, et al., 23
Placidyl, 126
Polansky, Norman, 15, 29, 61
Potential, 47, 75, 122, 127
Power, 15, 109
Practicality, 1, 47, 50, 51, 129
Prazepam, 121
Present, 5, 9, 13, 14, 15, 18, 19, 24, 25, 27, 28, 30, 35, 37, 46, 54, 56, 61, 63, 64, 69, 71–73, 78–81, 90–92, 95, 96, 98, 100, 101, 108, 113–16, 118, 119, 125, 127, 129
Problems, personal, 11, 16, 22, 24, 25, 28, 38, 39, 47, 51, 52, 55, 56, 63, 68, 73, 77, 83–86, 92, 105
Problems, situational, 24, 54
Problems, skin, 125
Professional, 7, 20, 23, 90–98, 100, 106, 107
Professional burnout, 7, 107
Professional ethics violation, 92
Projection, 67
Prolixin, 123
Promazine HCI, 123
Protriptyline, 120
Psychiatrists, forensic, 107
Psychologists, 107, 117
Psychosis, 67, 123, 128
Punish, 35, 78, 116, 117
Pushers, 77

Quide, 123

Rabkin, Richard, 16, 32, 41
Rachman, S., et al., 74, 77
Rank, Otto, 58, 62
Rashes, skin, 126
Real world, 4, 5, 12, 44, 45, 50, 69, 85, 105, 109
Reality, 7, 14, 49–51, 53, 57, 69, 83, 84, 98, 105, 109, 123
Referral sources, 95, 96, 101
Referrals, 95, 96
Relationship, 5, 51, 54, 55, 84
Relationship, intimate, 6, 21, 55, 84, 85, 92, 106
Relationships, 13, 14, 19, 78, 83–85, 113, 116, 118
Relationship factor, 14
Relationship skills, 11, 85
Relax, 74
Repoise, 123
Reserpine, 123
Resolution phase, 57, 62
Responsibilities, 98, 99, 110
Responsibility, 78, 89
Restoril, 126
Risk, 6, 15, 20, 34, 36, 52, 53, 62, 66, 73, 74, 83–85, 90, 101, 104, 124
Ritalin, 127
Rogers, Carl, 14, 55, 67, 86
Role confusion, 24
Roles, 10, 78, 81, 82
Runaway brain, 28

Schizoid, 26
Schizophrenics, 103
School, 9, 11, 12, 19, 21, 82, 95, 96, 101, 113, 118, 127
School and peer involvements, 9
Secobarbital, 126
Seconal, 126
Self, 6, 7, 10–15, 20, 23, 24, 26–41, 53, 54, 61, 65–67, 71, 73, 74, 76, 80–82, 86, 88, 96, 109, 112, 113, 116, 117, 121, 127
Self-appreciation, 13
Sensitization, 39
Serax, 121
Serentil, 123
Serpasil, 123
Sex, 67, 92, 107
Sex therapists, 107
Sexual dysfunction, 25
Sharing, 50, 85, 88, 89
Shepherd, 13, 33
Sifneos, P., 35, 70
Sinequan, 120
Skills, 5, 11–13, 15, 19, 28, 35, 58, 63, 65–67, 69, 70, 75, 83, 85, 91, 93, 96, 97, 107–10, 117
Social workers, 107
Sonnenburg, Stephen, et al., 13, 68
Sparine, 123
Specialization, 107
Spiritual, 12, 117
Spouse, 89
Stress, 24, 29, 59, 70, 71, 74, 77–79
Sublimation, 67
Substance abuse, 25, 26
Success, 7, 12, 15, 35, 36, 56, 66, 76, 77, 81, 84, 87, 96, 115
Successes, 19
Support, 7, 49, 50
Support system, 44
Support system, positive, 3, 11, 12, 14, 28, 30, 31, 33, 34, 36–38, 46, 51, 72, 82, 87, 95, 99, 102, 103, 106, 110, 113, 117
Suppression/repression, 67

Talbutal, 126
Talk, 88, 89, 112, 114, 116, 118
Talking, 34, 70, 88, 112
Taractan, 123
Teachers, 12, 21, 31, 32, 82
Tegretol, 125
Temazepam, 126
Tenuate, 127
Testing, 17, 22, 23, 62
Testing and written assessment, 22
Tests, personality, 22
Tests, targeted, 22, 45–47, 74, 81, 89
Therapeutic process, 20
Therapist, 1, 3–8, 13, 20, 22, 29, 98, 108, 109, 111
Therapy, individual, 43, 101, 109
Therapy, play, 101, 102
Therapy, short-term, 2–5, 8, 48–54, 60–63, 93, 111, 112
Therapy, supportive individual, 101
Think, 9, 10, 15, 23, 27–29, 31, 33, 34, 37, 38, 53–55, 70, 72, 88, 89, 97, 99, 112, 113, 116, 117
Thinking, creative, 15, 28, 36, 38, 39, 63, 66, 98
Thiorodazine, 123
Thiothixine, 123
Thought, 13, 28, 30, 33, 36, 37, 40, 41, 72, 76, 78, 106, 111, 112, 118, 123
Thought management, 36
Three to one rule, 37–38
Tindal, 123
Training, 1, 4, 5, 22, 37, 48, 65, 66, 87, 96, 108, 110, 119
Tranmep, 122
Transition, 60
Tranxene, 121
Tranylcypromine, 120

Trauma, 19, 24, 41, 42, 74
Trazodone, 120
Tremors, 125
Triazolam, 126
Triflupromazine, 123
Trilafon, 123
Trimethobenzamide, 123
Trimipramine, 120
Trust, 20, 22, 58, 61, 71, 89, 99, 102, 107, 113, 114, 118
Truth, 50, 53, 70, 92, 102, 118
Tuinal, 126
Tybamate, 121
Tybatran, 121

Upbringing, 9, 10

Valium, 122
Valmid, 126
Valproic acid, 124
Values, 4, 5, 10, 12, 74
Vengeance, 35
Verstran, 121
Vesprin, 123
Victim, 13, 81
Visotsky, Harold, 1
Vistaril, 121
Vivactil, 120
Vomiting, 126

Walker, Gillian, 14
Wedding, Danny, et al., 72
Weight gain, 125
White, Marjorie, et al., 72, 82, 84, 86, 89, 124
Widom, Cathy, 73, 78
Wirkin, Georgia, 78
Wolff, Sula, 10, 11, 18, 36, 51
Wolpe, Joseph, 18, 36, 51
Women, 73, 78, 79, 82
Work, 3, 4, 6, 10, 12, 15, 17, 21, 29, 34, 37, 51–53, 59, 65, 68, 70, 71, 76, 79, 83, 86, 92, 94, 97, 98, 101–4, 106–8, 110, 112–15, 121
Worry, 28, 29, 36, 37, 67, 97, 99, 119
Worship, 78

Xanax, 122

Yalom, 77